Mathematics
Practice Tests

Level 3
Mathematics

Michael W Priestley

Welcome to studySMART !

SCHOLASTIC

Mathematics Practice Tests is designed to help your child prepare to take mid-year and end-of-year tests.

Each practice test has 15 multiple-choice problems, 18–20 short response problems and 8–9 extended response problems. Your child should take 80–90 minutes to complete each practice test.

The questions in each test assess
- *Knowledge:* the ability to recall mathematical facts, concepts, rules and formulae, and to perform straightforward computations

- *Comprehension:* the ability to interpret data and use mathematical concepts, rules or formulae and to solve routine mathematical problems

- *Application and Analytical Skills:* the ability to analyze data and/or apply mathematical concepts, rules or formulae in complex situations

At the back of this book you will find a **Skills and Strategies Index** and an **Answer Key**.

The Skills and Strategies Index
- categorizes the problems according to Knowledge, Comprehension, and Application and Analytical Skills
- lists the mathematical concepts and skills measured and the test problems that measure each skill
- lists suggested problem-solving strategies for some extended response problems

This index may be helpful to you in determining what kinds of problems your child answered incorrectly, what skills he may be having trouble with, and which areas he may need further instruction in.

To score a test, please refer to the corresponding Answer Key, which lists the correct response to each problem and provides worked solutions to extended response problems.

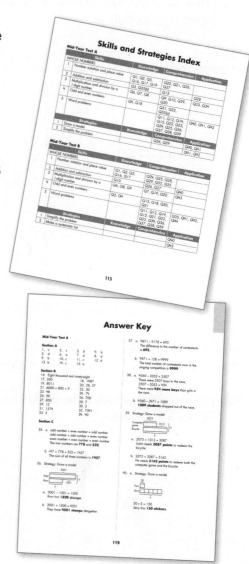

How to use this book

1. Ensure your child has the necessary tools such as a ruler, protractor, set-square etc.

2. Tell your child how much time he has to complete the practice test. Encourage him to work quickly and carefully, and to keep track of the remaining time — just as he would in a real testing session.

3. Do not allow your child to use a calculator.

4. To score a practice test, go through the test and mark each problem answered correctly. Add the number of correct answers to find your child's test score. Record the score on the contents page to keep track of your child's progress.
   You might want to have your child correct his own tests. This will give him a chance to see where he made mistakes and what he needs to do to improve his scores on the next test. Provide remediation as necessary.

5. Parallel problems across tests allow you to assess if remediation has been successful.

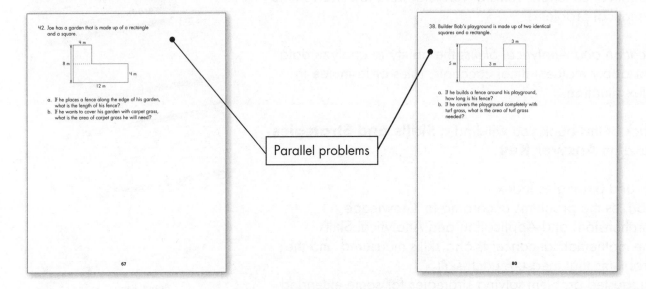

On the next page of this book, you will find test-taking tips. You may want to share these tips with your child before he begins working on the practice tests.

Note: To avoid the awkward 'he or she' construction, the pronouns on this page and in the parents' note will refer to the male gender.

A Note to Parents

Dear Parents

Children are more likely to be successful learners of mathematics when parents actively support their learning. By playing an active role in your child's learning, you will reinforce his skills and nurture a positive attitude towards mathematics.

Take some time to go through these test-taking strategies with your child so that he becomes familiar with them. Help your child apply these strategies when taking mathematics tests.

- **Learn the vocabulary**
  Become familiar with all mathematical terms that may appear in the test (for example *area*, *remainder*, *speed*, etc.) so that you understand what you are being asked to do.

- **Underline key words**
  Underline the key words after reading the problem carefully. Are you asked to find the sum? The angle measure?

- **Choosing the right option in a multiple-choice problem**
  Read the problem carefully then read all the answer options. Eliminate the options that you know are incorrect. If you are still unsure of the final answer, substitute the unknown in the problem with the remaining options and check if the answer is correct.

- **Identify the unnecessary information**
  Word problems sometimes give you more information than you need to solve the problem. Seek what you need and ignore the unnecessary information.

- **Use problem-solving strategies**
  Often there is more than one way to solve a problem. Apply a strategy that works best for a problem, e.g. drawing a picture, making a list, etc.

- **Use your time wisely**
  Plan how much time you should spend on each problem. This helps ensure that you have ample time to complete the test and do a thorough check of your work.

- **Check your work**
  When you have completed the test, go over as many problems as you can, making sure your answers are correct. Never rush through a mathematics test.

Contents

Topics Tested	Test Papers	Pages	Score
Mid-Year			
1. Number Notation and Place Value 2. Addition and Subtraction of Whole Numbers 3. Multiplication and Division of Whole Numbers 4. Odd and Even Numbers	Test A	7–20	50
	Test B	21–32	50
	Test C	33–42	50
	Test D	43–54	50

Topics Tested	Test Papers	Pages	Score
End-of-Year			
1. Number Notation and Place Value 2. Addition and Subtraction of Whole Numbers 3. Multiplication and Division of Whole Numbers 4. Odd and Even Numbers	Test E	56–68	50
5. Units of Measure 6. Addition, Subtraction, Multiplication and Division of Measures	Test F	69–82	50
7. Area and Perimeter 8. Bar Graphs 9. Equivalent Fractions 10. Comparing and Ordering Fractions 11. Addition and Subtraction of Fractions	Test G	83–98	50
12. Angles 13. Perpendicular and Parallel Lines	Test H	99–112	50

Skills and Strategies Index .... pages 113–118

Answer Key .... pages 119–128

Mid-Year Test A

Section A

Questions 1 to 15 carry 1 point each. For each question, choose the correct answer and write its letter in the parentheses ( ) provided.

1. A river is four thousand, one hundred and sixty kilometers long. Which is four thousand, one hundred and sixty as a numeral?
   a. 4016   b. 4106
   c. 4160   d. 4610   ( )

2. There are about 1850 kinds of beetles in a greenhouse. What does the digit 8 in 1850 stand for?
   a. 8 ones
   b. 8 tens
   c. 8 hundreds
   d. 8 thousands   ( )

3. Mr James took three flights.
   Singapore → Hong Kong:
                    2594 km
   Hong Kong → Thailand: 1658 km
   Thailand → Singapore: 1446 km

   How many kilometers did he fly in all?
   a. 4688 km   b. 4698 km
   c. 5688 km   d. 5698 km( )

4. The table shows the number of students in each teacher's class.

Name of teacher	Number of students
Mrs Alice	22
Ms Banu	27
Mrs Lee	28
Mr Ahmad	30

   Which teacher has an odd number of students in his or her class?
   a. Mrs Alice
   b. Ms Banu
   c. Mrs Lee
   d. Mr Ahmad   ( )

5. $8000 + 700 + 20 = \boxed{}$
   a. 8072   b. 1100
   c. 8702   d. 8720   ( )

6. $28 \times 10 = \boxed{}$
   a. 280   b. 281
   c. 290   d. 2810   ( )

7

7.
$$\begin{array}{r} 42 \\ \times\ 3 \\ \hline \square \end{array}$$

   a. 18   b. 26
   c. 45   d. 126   ( )

8.
$$\begin{array}{r} 75 \\ \times\ 4 \\ \hline \square \end{array}$$

   a. 260   b. 275
   c. 280   d. 300   ( )

9. $7 \times \square = 21$
   a. 2   b. 3
   c. 4   d. 6   ( )

10. $8 \times \square = 56$
   a. 5   b. 6
   c. 7   d. 8   ( )

11. Mr Rogers bought 32 pizzas for a school picnic. Each pizza was cut into 8 slices. How many slices of pizza were there in all?
   a. 40   b. 128
   c. 256   d. 266   ( )

12. A group of children visited a nursing home. There were 7 children in one mini-van and 8 children in another mini-van. Each child brought 4 self-made cards for the nursing home residents. How many cards did the children bring altogether?
   a. 15   b. 19
   c. 40   d. 60   ( )

13. If 1001 is added to a number and 2040 is subtracted from the result, the answer is 3961. What is the number?
   a. 1959   b. 5000
   c. 6039   d. 8041   ( )

14. Mr Lane bought 6 cartons of juice. Each carton had 24 cans of juice. Which number sentence should be used to find how many cans of juice he bought in all?
   a. $24 + 6 = \square$
   b. $24 - 6 = \square$
   c. $24 \times 6 = \square$
   d. $24 \div 6 = \square$ ( )

15. Last year, the population of Town Care was 8581. Since then, the population has grown by 1279 people. Which number sentence should be used to find the total population of Town Care now?

a. $8581 + 1279 = \square$

b. $8581 - 1279 = \square$

c. $8581 \times 1279 = \square$

d. $8581 \div 1279 = \square$ (   )

Section B

For questions 16 to 34, each answer carries 1 point. Write your answer in the answer blank provided.

16. Write the number 8098 in words.

Ans: _____

17. In 4278, what is the value of the digit 2?

Ans: _____

18. Which is an odd number, 1987 or 1978?

Ans: _____

19. What is the missing number in the pattern?

9011, $\square$, 7011, 6011

Ans: _____

20. What are the missing numbers in the number pattern?

25, ☐, 31, 34, ☐, 40

Ans: _____ and _____

21. Which has a greater value,
6000 + 80 + 9 or 6000 + 800 + 9?

Ans: _____

22. Rex had 37 badges. He collected 13 more badges.
How many badges did he have altogether?

Ans: _____ badges

23. In a box, there are 8 rows of bottles with 6 bottles in
each row. How many bottles are there in all?

Ans: _____ bottles

24. Jamal collected 592 ladybugs. He put them equally
into 8 tanks. How many ladybugs did he put in
each tank?

Ans: _____ ladybugs

25. A design on a towel has 351 petals on 9 stalks of flowers. If each stalk has the same number of petals, how many petals are there on each stalk?

Ans: _____ petals

26. What is the difference between 95 tens and 25 tens? Give your answer as a numeral.

Ans: _____

27. A 3-digit number can be divided by 10. The digit in the hundreds place is 8. The digit in the tens place is 5. What is the number?

Ans: _____

28. What is the missing digit?

```
    6  2  9  7
+   2  0  □  6
───────────────
    8  3  7  3
```

Ans: _____

The table shows a number pattern.
Use the table to answer questions 29 and 30.

48	36	24	A
8	6	4	B

29. What is the value of A?

Ans: _____

30. What is the value of B?

Ans: _____

Use the four digits shown to answer questions 31 and 32.

| 7 | 5 | 4 | 1 |

31. What is the smallest 4-digit even number that can be
    formed using all the digits?

Ans: _____

32. What is the greatest 4-digit odd number that can be
    formed using all the digits?

Ans: _____

Use the following to answer questions 33 and 34.

$\heartsuit \div 7 = \smiley$

$\smiley \times 3 = 15$

33. What is the value of $\smiley$?

Ans: _____

34. What is the value of $\smiley + \heartsuit$?

Ans: _____

Section C

For questions 35 to 42, each answer carries 1 point.
Write your answer in the space provided.
Show your work.

35. Three numbers are shown.

    147, 778, 532

    a. The sum of two of the numbers has an even digit in the ones place. Which are the two numbers?
    b. What is the sum of all three numbers?

36. Joey has 3001 stamps while Ross has 1501 fewer stamps than Joey.

    a. How many stamps does Ross have?
    b. How many stamps do they have altogether?

37. There are 9871 contestants in a singing competition.
The number of contestants in a dancing competition
has the digits 8 and 1 interchanged.

   a. What is the difference in the number
      of contestants?
   b. If another 128 contestants joined the singing
      competition, what is the number of contestants
      in the singing competition now?

38. A total of 4560 students took part in a race.

    a. If there were 2053 girls, how many more boys than girls were there in the race?

    b. If 3471 students finished the race, how many students dropped out of the race?

39. Justin requires 2075 points on his membership card to redeem a computer game. The computer game requires 1012 fewer points to redeem than a bicycle.

    a. How many points does Justin need to redeem the bicycle?

    b. How many points does he need to redeem both the computer game and the bicycle?

40. Tom has 30 stickers.
    Jerry has 5 times as many stickers as Tom.

    a. How many stickers does Jerry have?
    b. How many stickers must Jerry give to Tom so that
       both of them will have an equal number of stickers?

41. A mango costs 6 times as much as a pear.
I spend all my money on 3 mangoes and 12 pears.

   a. How many mangoes could I have bought with
      the same amount of money?
   b. How many pears could I have bought with the
      same amount of money?

42. A square table can seat 4 people. How many square tables are needed for 30 people, if the tables are joined from end to end?

Hint:

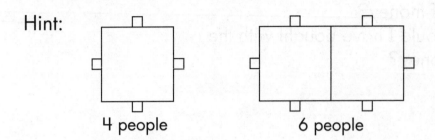

4 people   6 people

Mid-Year Test B

Section A

Questions 1 to 15 carry 1 point each. For each question, choose the correct answer and write its letter in the parentheses ( ) provided.

1. A lake is 1463 meters deep. What is 1463 in words?
   a. One thousand, three hundred and forty-six
   b. One thousand, four hundred and thirty-six
   c. One thousand, four hundred and sixty-three
   d. One thousand, six hundred and forty-three ( )

2. A total of 2945 people went to a hockey game. What does the digit 4 in 2945 stand for?
   a. 4 ones
   b. 4 tens
   c. 4 hundreds
   d. 4 thousands ( )

3. Which is an odd number?
   a. 1501   b. 2308
   c. 7336   d. 9420 ( )

4. Which street has an even number?
   a. Street 27   b. Street 39
   c. Street 15   d. Street 48 ( )

5. $2000 + 70 + 3 = \square$
   a. 273   b. 2073
   c. 2703   d. 2730 ( )

6. $54 \div 6 = \square$
   a. 6   b. 7
   c. 8   d. 9 ( )

7. $7 \times \square = 42$
   a. 6   b. 7
   c. 8   d. 9 ( )

8. $8\overline{)199}$
   a. 22 R1   b. 24
   c. 24 R7   d. 25 ( )

9.
$$519 \times 3 = \boxed{}$$

   a. 1534   b. 1537
   c. 1547   d. 1557 (   )

10. The table shows the number of visitors who went to an art show. How many visitors went to the art show in all?

Day	Number of visitors
Thursday	1271
Friday	1328
Saturday	1406

   a. 3005   b. 3995
   c. 4005   d. 4015 (   )

11. The owner of a miniature golf course bought 2 boxes of golf balls in June. Each box had 150 golf balls. By the end of August, 62 golf balls were lost. How many golf balls were left?
   a. 88   b. 90
   c. 238   d. 362 (   )

12. A group of 5 children went to the game arcade. Two children won 7 tokens each. The rest of the children won 4 tokens each. How many tokens did the group of children win in all?
   a. 12   b. 14
   c. 26   d. 28   (   )

13. Use all the four digits 5, 0, 2, 1 to form the smallest 4-digit even number.
   a. 1025   b. 1052
   c. 1205   d. 1250 (   )

14. Four people won a total of 1052 vouchers. Each person received an equal share of the prize. Which number sentence should be used to find the number of vouchers each person received?

   a. $1052 + 4 = \boxed{}$
   b. $1052 - 4 = \boxed{}$
   c. $1052 \times 4 = \boxed{}$
   d. $1052 \div 4 = \boxed{}$ (   )

15. McQueen drove for 36 hours last month. He used 6 liters of gasoline every hour while driving. Which question can you answer from this information?
a. How many different places did McQueen drive to?
b. What type of car does McQueen drive?
c. How much did each liter of gasoline cost?
d. How much gasoline did McQueen use last month?

( )

Section B

For questions 16 to 35, each answer carries 1 point.
Write your answer in the answer blank provided.

16. $6000 + 200 + 30 =$ ☐

Ans: _____

17. $9871 = 9000 + 800 +$ ☐ $+ 1$

Ans: _____

18. List all the odd numbers between 38 and 45.

Ans: _____

19. How many fives are there in 645?

Ans: _____

20. If $9 \times$ 😊 $= 900$, what is the value of 😊 $\times$ 😊?

Ans: _____

21. Kelly sold 69 muffins at a funfair and had 21 muffins left. How many muffins did she have at first?

Ans: _____ muffins

22. There are 9 cherries on each cake. How many cherries are there on 60 such cakes?

Ans: _____ cherries

23. There are 48 bags of birdseed in a box. Harry wants to place them equally in 6 smaller cartons. How many bags of birdseed will there be in each carton?

Ans: _____ bags

24. What is 16 hundreds more than 7801? Give your answer as a numeral.

Ans: _____

25. What is the difference in value between the digit 8 in 5018 and 2811?

Ans: _____

26. $8975 = 8000 + \boxed{} + 160 + 15$

Ans: _____

27. Subtract the sum of 3226 and 5436 from 9000. What is the answer?

Ans: _____

28. Take away 5 tens and 2 ones from 6 hundreds and 2 ones. What is the answer? Give your answer as a numeral.

Ans: _____

29. How many tens are there in the sum?

$1 + 2 + 3 + 4 + 5 + 6 + 7 + 8 + 9 = \boxed{}$

Ans: _____

Use the four digits below to answer questions 30 to 33.

| 6 | 5 | 1 | 2 |

30. What is the smallest 4-digit odd number that can be formed using all the digits?

Ans: _____

31. What is the greatest 4-digit even number that can be formed using all the digits?

Ans: _____

32. What is the difference between the greatest and smallest 4-digit numbers that can be formed using all the digits?

Ans: _____

33. How many different 4-digit numbers can be formed using these four digits?

Ans: _____

34. There are 8 packs of muesli bars in a box. Each pack has 5 muesli bars. Each bar has 2 almonds. How many almonds are there in the box?

Ans: _____ almonds

35. Three coupons are needed to redeem a bag of instant noodles. There are 5 packets of instant noodles in each bag. Spencer has 17 coupons. What is the greatest number of packets of noodles he can get?

Ans: _____ packets

Section C

For questions 36 to 44, each answer carries 1 point.
Write your answer in the space provided.
Show your work.

36. There were 5928 people at a rally.
    More people arrived at the rally an hour later.
    By interchanging the digit in the ones place with
    the digit in the thousands place in 5928, you get
    the total number of people at the rally.
    How many people arrived at the rally an hour later?

37. At an apple farm, Adam picked 2387 apples and
    June picked 2207 apples.

    a. How many apples did they pick altogether?
    b. How many more apples did Adam pick than June?

38. A total of 3500 people are seated at a concert.

   a. If 1109 of them are men, how many women
      are seated at the concert?
   b. If there are another 1340 people standing at
      the concert, what is the total number of people
      at the concert?

39. There are 200 blue hair clips and 300 red hair clips
    in a box.

   a. If Hannah packs all the hair clips into packets
      of 5, how many packets of hair clips will
      she have?
   b. If she buys 130 more red hair clips and repacks
      the hair clips into packets of 8, how many
      hair clips will be left unpacked?

40. What is the sum?
    21 + 22 + 23 + 37 + 38 + 39
    Hint: There is a shortcut to find the answer.

41. A bagel shop prepared 9 trays of bagels. There were
    32 bagels on each tray.

    a. How many bagels did the shop prepare?
    b. After 146 bagels were sold, the remainder was
       packed into boxes of 7 bagels each. How many
       bagels were not packed into boxes?

42. Vicky is 14 years old now. Six years ago, the sum of Vicky's age and her father's age was 50.

   a. How old is Vicky's father now?
   b. What is their total age now?

43. I am a 2-digit number. I am more than 13 but less than 26. I can be divided by both 4 and 5. What number am I?

44. For every 7 boxes of cereal bought, 3 muesli bars will be given free.

    a. If Brooke wants to get 9 free muesli bars, how many boxes of cereal must she buy?

    b. How many muesli bars will Brooke get if she buys 42 boxes of cereal?

Mid-Year Test C

Section A

Questions 1 to 15 carry 1 point each. For each question, choose the correct answer and write its letter in the parentheses ( ) provided.

1. Ms Grimes wrote this on the classroom board.

   ```
   Three thousand,
   nine hundred and ten
   ```

   Which number represents what she wrote on the board?
   a. 3019   b. 3091
   c. 3901   d. 3910   (   )

2. An art exhibition displayed 2651 works of art. What does the digit 2 in 2651 stand for?
   a. 2 ones
   b. 2 tens
   c. 2 hundreds
   d. 2 thousands   (   )

3. Which address has an even number?
   a. 31 Mill Road
   b. 45 First Avenue
   c. 59 Cane Road
   d. 60 Brook Street   (   )

4. $9000 + 600 + 50 = \boxed{}$
   a. 9056   b. 9065
   c. 9605   d. 9650   (   )

5. Ali took three flights.
   Singapore → Taiwan: 3247 km
   Taiwan → Thailand: 2529 km
   Thailand → Singapore: 1646 km

   How many kilometers did he travel in all?
   a. 6222 km   b. 6302 km
   c. 6422 km   d. 7422 km
   (   )

6. $15 \times 10 = \boxed{}$
   a. 150   b. 151
   c. 160   d. 1510   (   )

7.
   $$\begin{array}{r} 36 \\ \times\ 5 \\ \hline \boxed{} \end{array}$$

   a. 41   b. 150
   c. 170   d. 180   (   )

33

8.
$$60 \times 20 = \boxed{}$$

a. 120   b. 800
c. 1200   d. 1220   ( )

The table shows some of the highest mountains in the world. Use it to answer questions 9 and 10.

Mountain	Height (meters)
Manaslu	8163
Nanga Parbat	8126
Everest	8849
Annapurna	8090
Makalu	8484
K2	8610

9. Which is the highest mountain?
   a. K2
   b. Makalu
   c. Everest
   d Annapurna   ( )

10. Which mountain is taller than Makalu but shorter than Everest?
   a. K2
   b. Manaslu
   c. Annapurna
   d. Nanga Parbat   ( )

11. Which of these will result in an odd number?
   a. the sum of an odd number and an odd number
   b. the sum of an even number and an even number
   c. the sum of an odd number and an even number
   d. the product of an even number and an even number   ( )

12.
$$\begin{array}{r} 9\ 2\ 6\ 0 \\ -\ 2\ 6\ \boxed{}\ 4 \\ \hline 6\ 5\ 7\ 6 \end{array}$$

a. 1   b. 2
c. 8   d. 9   ( )

13. Rajah bought 45 garlic rolls for a party. Each roll was cut into 9 slices. How many slices were there in total?
   a. 5   b. 54
   c. 365   d. 405   ( )

14. An airplane can carry 395 passengers.
How many passengers can 4 such airplanes carry?
   a. 1185   b. 1480
   c. 1560   d. 1580   ( )

15. Five children sat in a row on a bench. Bob sat at one end. Lee sat between Bob and Jim. Pete sat next to Jim. Peggy sat next to Pete. Who sat at the other end?

    a. Peggy   b. Lee

    c. Pete   d. Jim   ( )

Section B

For questions 16 to 33, each answer carries 1 point. Write your answer in the answer blank provided.

16. In 6321, what is the value of the digit 3?

Ans: _____

17. List all the even numbers between 46 and 55.

Ans: _____

18. What is the missing number in the number pattern?

6011, 6021, 6031, ☐

Ans: _____

19. Which has a smaller value, 8000 + 70 + 1 or 8000 + 700 + 10?

Ans: _____

20. If $6 \times \diamond = 606$, what is the value of $\diamond$?

Ans: _____

21. How many sevens are there in 287?

Ans: _____

22. What is 12 tens less than 6218? Give your answer as a numeral.

Ans: _____

23. Add the difference between 3418 and 1260 to 5000. What is the answer?

Ans: _____

Use the numbers below to answer questions 24 and 25.

3136, 6619, 1223

24. The sum of two of the numbers has an even digit in the ones place. Which are the two numbers?

Ans: _____ and _____

25. The sum of two of the numbers has an even digit in the thousands place. Which are the two numbers?

Ans: _____ and _____

26. The numbers in the table form a pattern.

42	39	27	A
14	13	9	5

What is the value of A?

Ans: _____

27. A chipmunk collected 11 walnuts in the morning and 39 walnuts in the afternoon. How many walnuts did it collect altogether?

Ans: _____ walnuts

28. Bob arranged his matchbox car collection into 6 rows. Each row had 4 cars. How many cars did he have in his collection?

Ans: _____ cars

29. Mr Gan bought 72 erasers for his students. He divided the erasers equally among 8 groups of students. How many erasers did each group receive?

Ans: _____ erasers

30. There are 7 postcards and 7 envelopes in a packet. What is the total number of postcards and envelopes in 10 such packets?

Ans: _____ postcards and envelopes

31. The Singhs are driving from Malaysia to Thailand. The total distance is 2398 kilometers. They have traveled 1009 kilometers so far. How many more kilometers do they have to travel?

Ans: _____ km

32. A 3-digit number can be divided by 4. The digit in the hundreds place is 6 and the digit in the tens place is 6. What are the three possible 3-digit numbers?

Ans: _____, _____, or _____

33. The product of the 2 digits in a 2-digit number is 8. The sum of the tens and ones digit is 9. The tens digit is greater than the ones digit. What is the number?

Ans: _____

Section C

For questions 34 to 41, each answer carries 1 point.
Write your answer in the space provided.
Show your work.

34. Kelly scored 5561 points in a game while Mary scored 3451 fewer points than Kelly.

    a. How many points did Mary score?
    b. How many points did they score in total?

35. A farmer collected 3459 brown eggs and
    4229 white eggs.

    a. How many eggs are there in total?
    b. How many more white eggs than brown eggs
        are there?

36. Tom placed 410 cricket balls equally into 8 baskets.

    a. How many balls were there in each basket?
    b. How many balls were left behind?

37. There are 6127 people on Cruise Ship A. The number of people on Cruise Ship B has the digits 6 and 2 interchanged.

   a. What is the difference in the number of people on Cruise Ship A and Cruise Ship B?
   b. If another 873 people board Cruise Ship A, how many people are there on board now?

38. Renee is given the four digits below.

   | 6 | 1 | 0 | 5 |

   a. What is the greatest 4-digit even number she can form using all the digits?
   b. What is the difference between the greatest and smallest 4-digit numbers that she can form using all the digits?

39. Jack has 22 beans.
    Jill has 4 times as many beans as Jack.

    a. How many beans does Jill have?
    b. How many beans must Jill give to Jack so that
       they both will have an equal number of beans?

40. A book cost 5 times as much as a magazine.
    I bought 5 books and 6 magazines.

    a. How many books could I have bought for the
       same amount of money?
    b. How many magazines could I have bought for
       the same amount of money?

41. A rectangular table can seat 6 people.

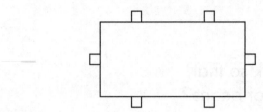

How many rectangular tables are needed for
26 people if the tables are joined end to end?

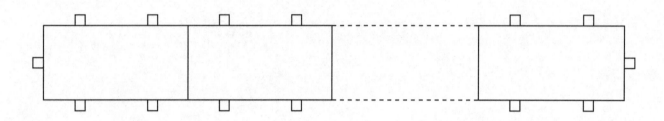

Mid-Year Test D

Section A

Questions 1 to 15 carry 1 point each. For each question, choose the correct answer and write its letter in the parentheses ( ) provided.

1. Mount Fuji in Japan is 3776 meters high.
   What is 3776 in words?
   a. Three thousand and seventy-six
   b. Three thousand, seven hundred and seven
   c. Three thousand, seven hundred and seventy-six
   d. Three thousand, six hundred and seventy ( )

2. There were 6952 people at the museum. What does the digit 5 in 6952 stand for?
   a. 5 ones
   b. 5 tens
   c. 5 hundreds
   d. 5 thousands ( )

3. Which sign has an odd number?
   a.
   Speed Limit
   60
   b.
   PAY TOLL
   500 m
   c.
   BOSTON
   31 km
   d.
   WALTON
   pop. 48
   ( )

4. $5000 + 100 + 60 + 2 = \boxed{}$

   a. 5126   b. 5162
   c. 5216   d. 5621 ( )

5.
   $7\overline{)35}$
   a. 4   b. 5
   c. 6   d. 7 ( )

6. $\begin{array}{r} 70 \\ \times\ 30 \\ \hline \square \end{array}$

   a. 100   b. 210
   c. 2100   d. 2900   ( )

7. $\begin{array}{r} 31 \\ \times\ 6 \\ \hline \square \end{array}$

   a. 37   b. 96
   c. 156   d. 186   ( )

8. $\begin{array}{r} 208 \\ \times\ 4 \\ \hline \square \end{array}$

   a. 212   b. 632
   c. 832   d. 872   ( )

9. The table shows the number of children who entered Fantasyland Park on three days.

Day	Number of children
Saturday	2232
Sunday	3567
Monday	1125

How many children entered the park in total?
a. 6814   b. 6824
c. 6914   d. 6924   ( )

10. Which number sentence will have a result that is an even number?

   a. $3 + 5 + 7 = \square$

   b. $10 + 0 = \square$

   c. $11 - 5 - 3 = \square$

   d. $7 - 0 = \square$ ( )

11. In Jamie's garden, there are 5 rows of sunflowers. There are 7 sunflowers in each row. How many sunflowers are there in all?
a. 12   b. 25
c. 35   d. 42   ( )

12. Grace is reading a series of books that has 4750 pages in total. She read 1003 pages two months ago, 1200 pages last month, and 1256 pages this month. How many pages does she have left to read?
a. 1291   b. 1301
c. 1309   d. 1341   ( )

13. Bob bought 8 crates of grape juice. Each crate has 32 bottles. Which number sentence should be used to find how many bottles of grape juice he bought in all?

   a. $32 + 8 = \square$

   b. $32 - 8 = \square$

   c. $32 \times 8 = \square$

   d. $32 \div 8 = \square$ ( )

14. ☺ × ☺ = ✲

☺ + ☺ + ☺ + ☺ = ✲

What does ✲ represent?

a. 4　　　　b. 16

c. 25　　　　d. 36　　　　(　)

15. Stan makes a tower of 5 blocks. The yellow block is at the bottom and the blue block is at the top. The red block is between the blue and white blocks. The green block is below the white block but above the yellow block. Which color block is at the top of the tower?

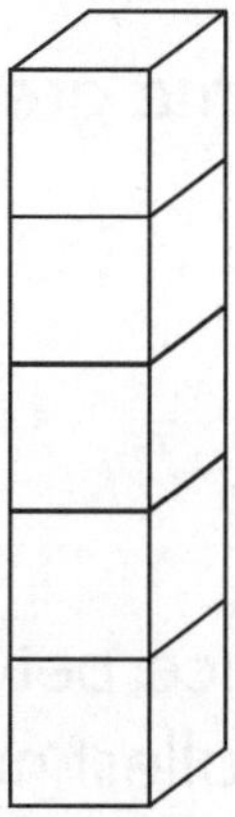

a. red　　　　b. green

c. white　　　　d. blue　　　　(　)

Section B

For questions 16 to 35, each answer carries 1 point.
Write your answer in the answer blank provided.

16. Write the number 5011 in words.

Ans: ______________________________

17. 7025 = ☐ + 20 + 5

Ans: ____________

Use the four numbers shown to answer questions 18 to 20.

| 15 | 127 | 11 | 102 |

18. Which is an even number?

Ans: _____

19. What is the sum of the greatest and the smallest number?

Ans: _____

20. What is the difference between the greatest even number and the smallest number?

Ans: _____

21. Form the greatest 4-digit odd number using all the digits shown.

3, 0, 4, 1

Ans: _____

22. Form the smallest 4-digit even number using all the digits shown.

7, 8, 0, 2

Ans: _____

23. List all the even numbers between 75 and 89.

    Ans: _____

24. How many fours are there in 448?

    Ans: _____

25. What is the product of 125 and 4?

    Ans: _____

26. What is 25 tens more than 7021?
    Give your answer as a numeral.

    Ans: _____

27. What is the difference in value between the digit 5
    in 2519 and 3057?

    Ans: _____

28. Which has a greater value,
    1000 + 160 + 25 or 1000 + 100 + 65?

    Ans: _____

29. Add 8107 to the difference between 5329
    and 4128. What is the answer?

    Ans: _____

30. 7000 + ☐ + 200 + 60 = 7967

    Ans: _____

31. There were 171 girls and 209 boys in a park.
How many children were there in the park in all?

Ans: _____ children

32. Joe had 25 buns. He bought another 35 buns and
put the buns equally onto 4 serving plates.
How many buns were on each plate?

Ans: _____ buns

33. Add 1 thousand, 6 hundreds and 5 ones to
5 thousands, 12 tens and 6 ones. What is
the answer? Give your answer as a numeral.

Ans: _____

34. I am a number.
I am less than 35 but more than 12.
I can be divided exactly by 4 and 10.
What am I?

Ans: _____

35. What numeral does Ω represent?

```
    4   2   Ω   5
+   2   Ω   3   Ω
_____
    6   9   0   1
```

Ans: _____

48

Section C

For questions 36 to 43, each answer carries 1 point.
Write your answer in the space provided.
Show your work.

36. There were 600 computers in a storeroom.
    After a flood, 235 computers were destroyed.

    a. How many computers were not destroyed?
    b. If the computers that were not destroyed were
       packed into crates of 5 computers each, how
       many crates were there?

37. Every pack of baseball cards came with 2 free stickers.
    Sophie wanted to collect 48 stickers.

    a. How many packs of baseball cards did Sophie
       need to buy?
    b. If she had already bought 16 packs of baseball
       cards, how many more packs did she need to buy?

38. On Monday, 3560 tarts were baked at a bakery.
    1135 fewer tarts were baked on Tuesday.

    a. How many tarts were baked on Tuesday?
    b. How many tarts in total were baked on both days?

39. A farmer packs 40 boxes into a crate. Each box has
    4 pineapples. If the farmer has 7 crates, how many
    pineapples does he pack?

40. Eight years ago, Minah was 10 years old.
   Today, the sum of her age and her mother's age
   is 60 years.

   a. How old is Minah's mother today?
   b. What was their total age 8 years ago?

41. A customer gets 2 bars of soap for free for every 6 bars that he buys.

   a. How many bars of soap does a customer get for free if he buys 36 bars of soap?

   b. If a customer wants to get a total of 32 bars of soap, how many bars of soap does he need to buy?

42. Sue is given the four digits shown.

| 3 | 6 | 2 | 8 |

She uses all the digits to form different 4-digit numbers.

a. How many different 4-digit numbers can she form?
b. What is the difference between the greatest and the smallest 4-digit numbers?

43. There are a total of 66 cars and motorcycles in a parking garage. A mechanic counts 204 wheels in all.

   a. How many motorcycles are there?
   b. Half the cars and some motorcycles are removed. If there are 112 wheels now, how many motorcycles were removed?

Date: _____

End-of-Year Test E

Section A

Questions 1 to 15 carry 1 point each. For each question, choose the correct answer and write its letter in the parentheses ( ) provided.

1. Which address has an even number?
   a. Block 95
   b. Avenue 15
   c. Street 27
   d. Avenue 6   (   )

2. The table shows the population in six towns.

Town	Population
A	2344
B	3190
C	1519
D	3478
E	1792
F	2876

   Which town has the most number of people?
   a. Town A   b. Town B
   c. Town D   d. Town F   (   )

3. $32 \times 10 = \boxed{}$
   a. 230   b. 320
   c. 321   d. 2310   (   )

4. $\begin{array}{r} 85 \\ \times\ 4 \\ \hline \boxed{} \end{array}$
   a. 34   b. 320
   c. 340   d. 3440   (   )

5. What is the missing number in the pattern?
   23, 30, 38, 47, $\boxed{}$
   a. 54   b. 55
   c. 56   d. 57   (   )

6. The figure is made up of 1-centimeter squares.

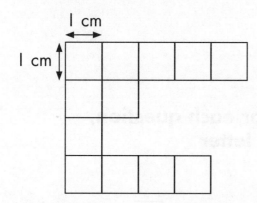

   What is the area of the figure?
   a. 9 cm²   b. 12 cm²
   c. 17 cm²   d. 20 cm²   (   )

The bar graph shows the amount of snowfall in the winter of 2010–2011. Use the graph to answer questions 7 and 8.

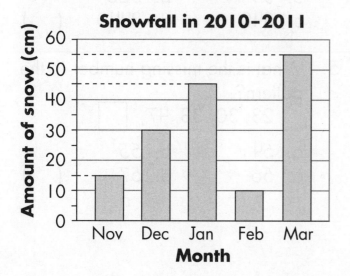

7. In which month was the amount of snowfall the greatest?
   a. November
   b. January
   c. February
   d. March   (   )

8. What was the amount of snowfall in December?
   a. 10 cm   b. 15 cm
   c. 30 cm   d. 45 cm   (   )

9.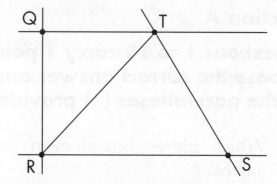

   Which line segment is perpendicular to $\overline{QT}$?
   a. $\overline{RT}$ b. $\overline{TS}$
   c. $\overline{RS}$ d. $\overline{QR}$ (   )

Use the diagram to answer questions 10 and 11.

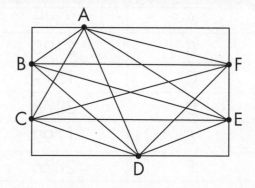

10. Which line segment is parallel to line segment BF?
    a. $\overline{AD}$ b. $\overline{BD}$
    c. $\overline{CE}$ d. $\overline{CF}$ (   )

11. Which is a right angle?
    a. ∠ABF   b. ∠BCE
    c. ∠DEF   d. ∠BCD   (   )

56

12. At a bake sale, 8567 cookies were on sale. 3456 cookies were sold in the morning and 3667 cookies were sold in the afternoon. How many cookies were left?
a. 211　　　b. 1444
c. 5111　　　d. 7123　　(　)

13. Josh bought 5 boxes of golf balls. Each box had 12 balls. Which number sentence should be used to find how many golf balls he bought in all?
a. $12 + 5 = \square$
b. $12 - 5 = \square$
c. $12 \times 5 = \square$
d. $12 \div 5 = \square$　　(　)

14. Lance rode his motorcycle across the country. The trip took 64 days. How many weeks did the trip last?
a. 6 weeks 4 days
b. 8 weeks 6 days
c. 9 weeks 1 day
d. 10 weeks　　　　　　(　)

15. Selena was 1 meter 55 centimeters tall last year. Since then, she has grown 8 centimeters. How tall is she now?
a. 1 m 47 cm
b. 1 m 58 cm
c. 1 m 63 cm
d. 2 m 3 cm　　　　　　(　)

57

Section B

For questions 16 to 35, each answer carries 1 point.
Write your answer in the answer blank provided.

16. There are about 1370 kinds of spiders in Friendly Forest. What does the digit 3 in 1370 stand for?

Ans: _____

17. How many hundreds are there in 7821?

Ans: _____ hundreds

18.   86
    × 6
    ⬚

Ans: _____

19. What are the values of A, B, and C?

$$\frac{4}{5} = \frac{A}{10} = \frac{12}{B} = \frac{C}{20}$$

Ans: _____, _____, and _____

20. 163 red beans are mixed with 279 green beans. How many beans are there in all?

Ans: _____ beans

Use the map to answer questions 21 and 22.

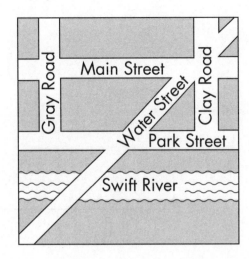

21. Which street is parallel to Main Street?

Ans: _____

22. Which road is parallel to Clay Road?

Ans: _____

Use the picture below to answer questions 23 and 24.

23. How many angles are there on the sticker?

Ans: _____

24. How many pairs of parallel sides are there on the sticker?

Ans: _____

25. What is the area of a square with sides measuring 2 centimeters each?

2 cm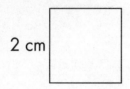

Ans: _____ cm^2

26. Which circle is $\frac{2}{3}$ shaded?

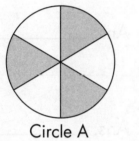
Circle A

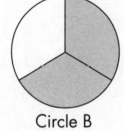
Circle B

Ans: Circle _____

27. What fraction of the figure is shaded?

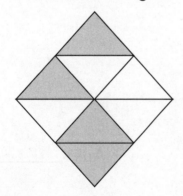

Ans: _____

The bar graph below shows the amount of lemonade produced by five factories in 2011.

Use the graph to answer questions 28 and 29.

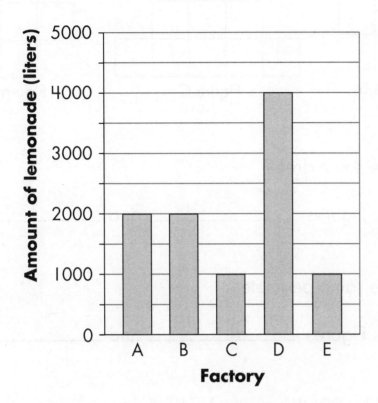

28. Which factory produced the most lemonade?

Ans: Factory _____

29. What is the difference between the greatest and the least amount of lemonade produced?

Ans: _____ L

Use figures A to D to answer questions 30 and 31.

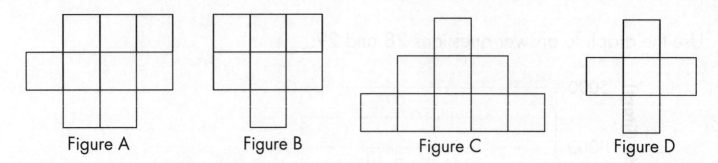

Figure A   Figure B   Figure C   Figure D

30. Which two figures have the same area?

Ans: Figures _____ and _____

31. Which two figures have the same perimeter?

Ans: Figures _____ and _____

32. When a number is divided by 12, the quotient is 4.
    What is the quotient if the same number is divided
    by 8?

Ans: _____

33. What is the value of A?

$$\frac{6}{9} = \frac{A}{6}$$

Ans: _____

34. Arrange the numbers in order. Begin with the greatest.

$$\frac{2}{7}, \ 1, \ \frac{3}{5}, \ \frac{2}{4}$$

Ans: _____, _____, _____, _____

35. Arrange the fractions in order. Begin with the smallest.

$$\frac{6}{8}, \ \frac{9}{10}, \ \frac{6}{9}, \ \frac{4}{5}$$

Ans: _____, _____, _____, _____

Section C

**For questions 36 to 43, each answer carries 1 point.
Write your answer in the space provided.
Show your work.**

36. A fruit seller has 736 pears in a box.

    a. How many pears are there in 6 boxes?
    b. He packs the pears equally into 5 large
       crates. How many pears are left?

37. Leena has 750 grams of flour.
    She uses 260 grams of it.

    a. How much flour is left?
    b. If she packs the remaining flour into 2 bags equally, what is the mass of flour in each bag?

38. Jack has $\frac{3}{5}$ liter of fruit juice. Jill has $\frac{1}{10}$ liter of fruit juice.

    a. How much fruit juice do they have altogether?
    b. If they buy another $\frac{3}{10}$ liter of fruit juice, how much fruit juice do they have in all?

39. There was $\frac{2}{3}$ liter of milk in a jug.

Jack used $\frac{1}{6}$ liter of milk for baking.

   a. How much milk was left?

   b. If he spilled $\frac{1}{12}$ liter of milk, how much milk did

       he have finally?

40. A rectangular garden has a length of 43 meters and a breadth of 28 meters. A wire fence is placed along the edge of the garden.

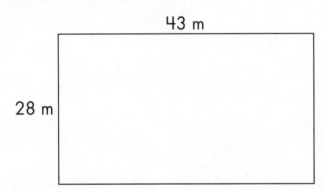

   a. What is the length of the wire fence?

   b. What is the area of the garden?

41. Linda recorded the amount of time she spent on her science fair project over four days.

Day	Time spent
Monday	43 min
Tuesday	1 hour 10 min
Wednesday	24 min
Thursday	$1\frac{1}{2}$ hours

a. How much time did Linda spend on her project altogether? Give your answer in hours and minutes.

b. How much more time did she spend on her project on Tuesday than on Wednesday?

42. Joe has a garden that is made up of a rectangle and a square.

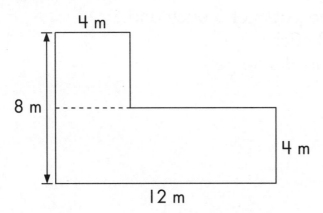

a. If he places a fence along the edge of his garden, what is the length of his fence?

b. If he wants to cover his garden with carpet grass, what is the area of carpet grass he will need?

43. Matt bought 4 boxes of keychains.
Each box contained 200 keychains.
He repacked half of them into packs of 5 each and
the other half into packs of 8 each.
How many packs of keychains did he get?

End-of-Year Test F

Section A

Questions 1 to 15 carry 1 point each. For each question, choose the correct answer and write its letter in the parentheses ( ) provided.

1. Write six thousand and seventy-two as a numeral.
   a. 672   b. 6072
   c. 6702   d. 6720   (   )

2. Which is an even number?
   a. 1847   b. 2345
   c. 3789   d. 5636   (   )

3. What is the area of the figure?

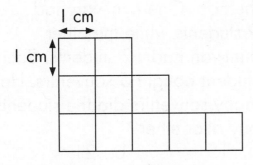

   a. 6 cm²   b. 8 cm²
   c. 10 cm²   d. 12 cm²   (   )

4. What is the area of the figure?

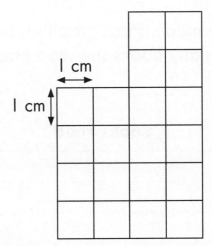

   a. 4 cm²   b. 16 cm²
   c. 20 cm²   d. 64 cm²   (   )

5.

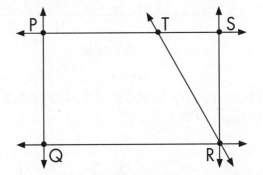

Which line is parallel to $\overleftrightarrow{PS}$?
   a. $\overleftrightarrow{PQ}$ b. $\overleftrightarrow{TR}$
   c. $\overleftrightarrow{SR}$ d. $\overleftrightarrow{QR}$ (   )

6.

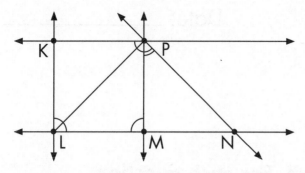

Which angle measures less than 90°?

a. ∠MPN   b. ∠KLM

c. ∠KPN   d. ∠PML   ( )

7. Adele made a bar graph to show how many books she read each week.

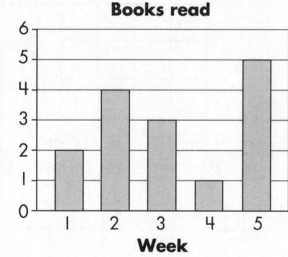

Books read

How many books did she read in Week 2?

a. 2   b. 3

c. 4   d. 5   ( )

8. Six farmers shared 9174 seeds equally. Which number sentence should be used to find the number of seeds each farmer gets?

a. 9174 + 6 = ☐

b. 9174 – 6 = ☐

c. 9174 × 6 = ☐

d. 9174 ÷ 6 = ☐   ( )

9. Janice bought 3 boxes of ice-cream sticks. Each box had 120 ice-cream sticks. She gave 51 sticks to her students. How many ice-cream sticks were left?

a. 69   b. 171

c. 309   d. 360   ( )

10. Mrs Jacobs took her students to the zoo. One mini-van had 9 students while the other mini-van had 12 students. Each student bought 5 souvenirs. How many souvenirs did the students buy altogether?

a. 15   b. 21

c. 105   d. 540   ( )

11. Which shows the fractions arranged from the greatest to the smallest?

a. $\dfrac{3}{10}, \dfrac{3}{5}, \dfrac{1}{2}, \dfrac{1}{4}$

b. $\dfrac{3}{5}, \dfrac{1}{2}, \dfrac{3}{10}, \dfrac{1}{4}$

c. $\dfrac{1}{4}, \dfrac{1}{2}, \dfrac{3}{10}, \dfrac{3}{5}$

d. $\dfrac{1}{2}, \dfrac{1}{4}, \dfrac{3}{5}, \dfrac{3}{10}$ (   )

12. A bag of 18 pears is most likely to have a mass of _____.
    a. 3 grams
    b. 3 liters
    c. 3 milliliters
    d. 3 kilograms   (   )

13. Liam traveled for 4 weeks and 4 days. How many days did Liam travel?
    a. 24   b. 28
    c. 30   d. 32   (   )

14. Mrs Coombs is watching a television show that lasts 60 minutes. She has been watching for 48 minutes. How much longer will the show last?
    a. 10 min   b. 12 min
    c. 22 min   d. 24 min   (   )

15. Roland started soccer practice at 3.30 p.m. and played for $2\dfrac{1}{2}$ hours. What time did he finish soccer practice?
    a. 6 p.m.   b. 6.30 p.m.
    c. 7 p.m.   d. 8 p.m.   (   )

Section B

For questions 16 to 33, each answer carries 1 point. Write your answer in the answer blank provided.

16. A bookstore has 5672 comic books. What does the digit 7 in 5672 stand for?

Ans: _____

17. A singer received 2567 letters in the mail last year. How many hundreds was that?

Ans: _____ hundreds

18. $75 \times 5 = \square$

Ans: _____

19. What are the values of A, B, and C?

$$\frac{3}{4} = \frac{12}{A} = \frac{B}{8} = \frac{15}{C}$$

Ans: _____, _____, and _____

20.

Which line is parallel to $\overleftrightarrow{AB}$?

Ans: _____

21. How many angles are there in this figure?

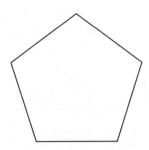

Ans: _____

22. Is ∠ADC greater or less than a right angle?

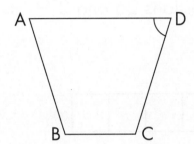

Ans: _____

23. Which figure is $\frac{1}{4}$ shaded?

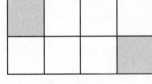

Figure A

Figure B

Ans: Figure _____

24. What fraction of the figure is shaded?

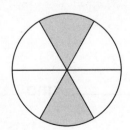

Ans: _____

25. Which object is about 1-meter long?

umbrella   pick-up truck   egg   shoe

Ans: _____

Use the figures P, Q, R, and S to answer questions 26 and 27.

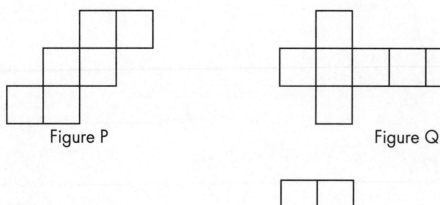

Figure P   Figure Q

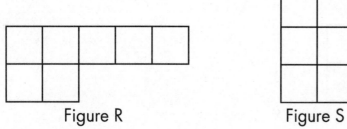

Figure R   Figure S

26. Which two figures have the same area?

Ans: Figures _____ and _____

27. Which two figures have the same perimeter?

Ans: Figures _____ and _____

The bar graph shows the favorite colors of some students.
Use the graph to answer questions 28 and 29.

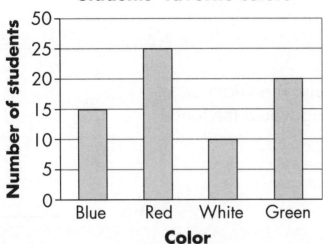

Students' favorite colors

28. Which is the most popular color?

Ans: _____

29. What is the difference between the number of students who like the most popular color and the least popular color?

Ans: _____

30. $\dfrac{2}{10} = \dfrac{3}{\boxed{}}$

Ans: _____

31. Arrange the fractions in order. Begin with the smallest.

$$\frac{3}{4}, \frac{3}{6}, \frac{6}{13}, \frac{5}{5}$$

Ans: _____, _____, _____, _____

32. A tank can hold 22 liters of water. Each liter of water has a mass of 1 kilogram. How many kilograms of water can the tank hold?

Ans: _____ kg

33. Mr Marcus has 48 fencing panels. The width of each panel is 5 meters. How long would the fence be if he used all the panels?

Ans: _____ m

Section C

For questions 34 to 42, each answer carries 1 point.
Write your answer in the space provided.
Show your work.

34. The bar graph shows the number of visitors who attended a flower exhibition.

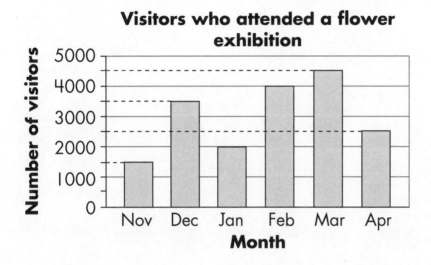

Visitors who attended a flower exhibition

a. What was the highest number of visitors to the exhibition in a month?

b. If each visitor is given 2 flowers, what is the difference in the number of flowers given between January and February?

35. Mrs Marsh gave 8 pencils to each student in a group of 6 boys and 3 girls.

    a. How many pencils did she give to her students in total?

    b. If she gave each student 7 pencils instead, how many pencils would be left over?

36. Kim added $\frac{1}{8}$ liter of syrup to $\frac{3}{4}$ liter of water to make fruit punch.

    a. How many liters of fruit punch did she make?

    b. How many more liters of water than syrup did she use?

37. When Mr Gomez gives all the crayons in a box to
9 students equally, each student receives 7 crayons.
If he wants to give each student 9 crayons instead,
how many crayons is he short of?

38. Builder Bob's playground is made up of two identical squares and a rectangle.

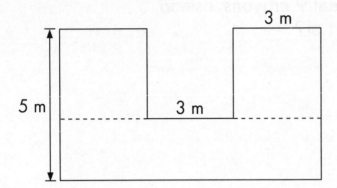

a. If he builds a fence around his playground, how long is his fence?
b. If he covers the playground completely with turf grass, what is the area of turf grass needed?

39. Mona mixes $\frac{1}{2}$ kilogram of flour with $\frac{1}{6}$ kilogram of sugar and $\frac{1}{12}$ kilogram of butter.

    a. How much more sugar than butter is there?
    b. What is the total mass of the mixture?

40. After school, Randy spent $2\frac{1}{2}$ hours at soccer practice. Then, he spent 25 minutes on his spelling homework, 40 minutes on math problems, and $1\frac{1}{2}$ hours on a social studies project.

    a. How much time did Randy spend on all his homework?
    b. How much more time did Randy spend on all his homework than on soccer?

41. Kim bought 4 large boxes of pencils.
Each box contained 105 pencils.
She repacked a third of them into packs of 7 each
and the rest into packs of 8 each.
How many packs of pencils did she have?

42. A farmer has a total of 20 chickens and sheep.
The animals have 56 legs in all.
How many of these animals are chickens and how
many are sheep?

End-of-Year Test G

Section A

Questions 1 to 15 carry 1 point each. For each question, choose the correct answer and write its letter in the parentheses ( ) provided.

1. $9000 + 600 + 50 = \boxed{}$
    a. 9065   b. 9560
    c. 9605   d. 9650   (   )

2. Which is an odd number?
    a. 1102   b. 2060
    c. 3481   d. 7254   (   )

Use the map to answer questions 3 and 4.

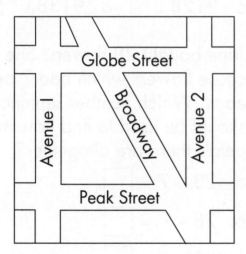

3. Which two streets are parallel?
    a. Avenue 1 and Peak Street
    b. Globe Street and Peak Street
    c. Avenue 1 and Broadway
    d. Globe Street and Avenue 2
    (   )

4. Which two streets form a right angle with each other?
    a. Avenue 2 and Peak Street
    b. Globe Street and Peak Street
    c. Avenue 1 and Broadway
    d. Broadway and Globe Street
    (   )

The bar graph shows the attendance at hockey games played by the Cougars each month.
Use the graph to answer questions 5 and 6.

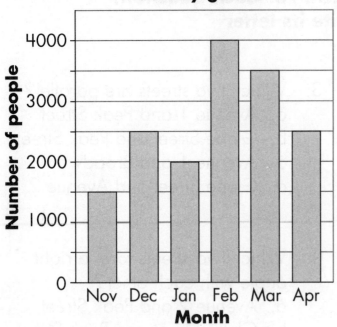

Attendance at Cougars' hockey games

5. In which month did the most number of people attend the hockey games?
   a. December   b. January
   c. February   d. March   (   )

6. How many people attended the hockey games in April?
   a. 1500   b. 2000
   c. 2500   d. 3000   (   )

7. What is the missing number in the number pattern?

   176, 157, 138, 119, ☐

   a. 80   b. 90
   c. 99   d. 100   (   )

8. The table shows the amount of milk Dave, the Grocer ordered for his shop on three days.

Day	Amount of milk (liters)
Monday	1254
Wednesday	1428
Friday	1456

How much milk did he order altogether?
   a. 3138 L   b. 4038 L
   c. 4128 L   d. 4138 L   (   )

9. Jane bought 28 flowers. She chose flowers which had 7 petals each. Which number sentence should be used to find how many petals there are altogether?

   a. $28 + 7 = $ ☐

   b. $28 - 7 = $ ☐

   c. $28 \times 7 = $ ☐

   d. $28 \div 7 = $ ☐   (   )

10. Susan's father wants to fence up their garden which is in the shape of a square.

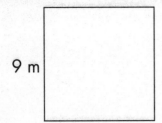

9 m

What is the length of fencing he needs to buy?
a. 9 m
b. 18 m
c. 36 m
d. 81 m   (   )

11. What is the area of the figure? Each square has sides measuring 2 centimeters.

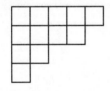

a. 44 cm²
b. 48 cm²
c. 52 cm²
d. 60 cm²   (   )

12. Which unit should be used to measure the length of a living room?
a. millimeters
b. centimeters
c. meters
d. kilograms   (   )

13. A bathtub that is filled with water would hold about how many liters of water?

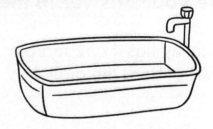

a. 3 L
b. 30 L
c. 300 L
d. 3000 L (   )

14. Justin started playing a computer game at 1.15 p.m. and stopped playing at 3.40 p.m. For how long did he play the game?
a. 2 h 15 min
b. 2 h 25 min
c. 2 h 35 min
d. 3 h 5 min   (   )

15. Bill started watching a video at 9.30 a.m. The video lasted 80 minutes. At what time did the video end?
a. 9.50 a.m.
b. 10.30 a.m.
c. 10.40 a.m.
d. 10.50 a.m.   (   )

Section B

For questions 16 to 33, each answer carries 1 point.
Write your answer in the answer blank provided.

16. Timmy has 1752 marbles in his collection.
What does the digit 1 in 1752 stand for?

Ans: _____

17. Baker John baked 1761 bagels.
How many tens is that?

Ans: _____ tens

18. 30 × 8 = ☐

Ans: _____

19. 23 × 15 = ☐

Ans: _____

20. There are 38 black beads and 32 white beads in a bag.
How many beads are there in total?

Ans: _____ beads

21. What are the missing numbers?

$\frac{1}{2} = \frac{\boxed{}}{4} = \frac{\boxed{}}{10} = \frac{\boxed{}}{20}$

Ans: _____, _____, and _____

22. How many angles can be found within the figure?

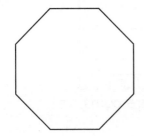

Ans: _____

23. Which figure is $\frac{2}{5}$ shaded?

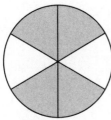 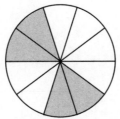

Figure A   Figure B

Ans: Figure _____

24. What fraction of the figure is shaded?

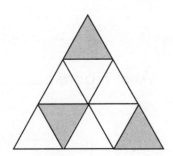

Ans: _____

25. Jessica collected keychains, magnets, stamps, and rare coins. The bar graph shows the number of each item that she has collected.

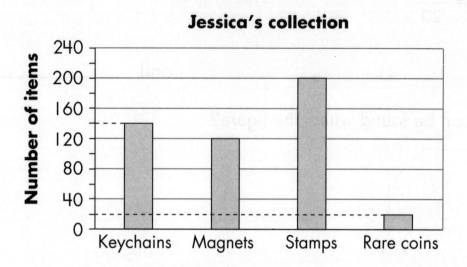

How many number of items does Jessica have in her collection altogether?

Ans: _____ items

Use the figures X, Y, and Z shown to answer questions 26 and 27.

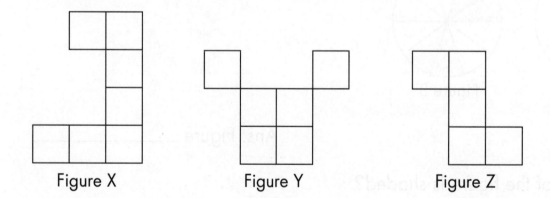

Figure X   Figure Y   Figure Z

26. Which figure has the greatest area?

Ans: Figure _____

27. Which figure has the smallest perimeter?

Ans: Figure _____

Use the square shown to answer questions 28 and 29.

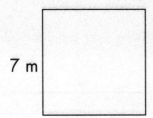

7 m

28. What is the area of the square?

Ans: _____ m²

29. What is the perimeter of 2 similar squares placed side by side?

Ans: _____ m

30. When a number is divided by 6, the quotient is 16. What is the quotient if the number is divided by 8?

Ans: _____

31. What is the value of A?

$$\frac{10}{12} = \frac{15}{A}$$

Ans: _____

32. Arrange the fractions in order. Begin with the smallest.

$$\frac{6}{6}, \frac{5}{10}, \frac{3}{9}, \frac{3}{4}$$

Ans: _____, _____, _____, _____

33. Find the area of a rectangular path 3 meters wide in a garden that is 12 meters wide and 17 meters long.

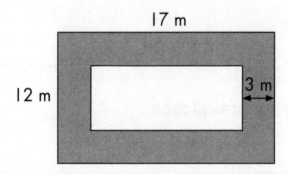

Ans: _____ m²

Section C

For questions 34 to 41, each answer carries 1 point.
Write your answer in the space provided.
Show your work.

34. A sticker album has 22 pages filled with stickers.
Each page displays 100 stickers.

    a. How many stickers are there in the album?

    b. If Jack removes all the stickers and pastes them
equally on 11 pages, how many stickers does
he paste on each page?

35. There are 38 students in each class of Grade 6.
    There are 12 Grade 6 classes altogether.

    a. How many students are there altogether?

    b. How many more students need to join the school
    in order to have 10 classes of 46 students each?

36. Mrs Raj used $\frac{1}{6}$ kilogram of flour for tarts and $\frac{1}{2}$ kilogram of flour for pies.

    a. How much flour did she use in all?

    b. How much more flour did she use for the pies than the tarts?

37. The table shows the type of transport the people from four towns take to work each morning.

Town	A	B	C	D
Bus	51	49	63	37
Car	15	47	17	21
Subway	92	36	118	54
Taxi	10	15	8	17

a. How many people from the four towns take the subway altogether?
b. Use the table to complete the bar graph.

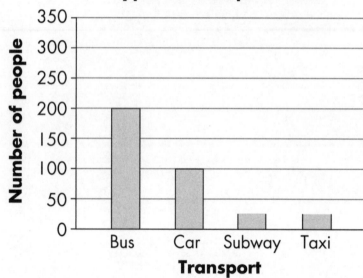

Types of transport taken

38. Tim has a lemonade stand. The table shows how much lemonade he sold each day.

Day	Lemonade sold (liters)
Wednesday	$\frac{1}{4}$
Thursday	$\frac{2}{3}$
Friday	$\frac{1}{6}$
Saturday	$\frac{3}{4}$

a. On which day did Tim sell the most lemonade?
b. How much lemonade did he sell altogether on Thursday and Friday?

39. Rose cut out a piece of cardboard that is made up of a square and rectangle.

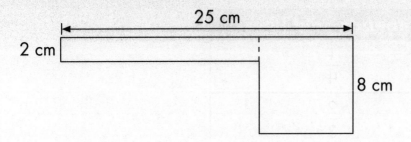

a. If she wants to place a ribbon all around the cardboard, what is the length of ribbon she needs?
b. If she wants to cover the cardboard with a plastic sheet, what is the area of plastic sheet she needs?

40. On the first day, Hank braided 3 meters of rope. By the second day, he finished braiding 500 centimeters of the rope. By the third day, he finished braiding 8 meters of the rope. By the fourth day, he finished braiding 1200 centimeters of the rope. He continued in this increasing pattern until he finished braiding the length of the rope.

   a. By which day would he have braided 38 meters of the rope?
   b. If he took 12 days to finish braiding, how long was the rope in the end?

41. The street facing Kimberly's house has 16 trees. There is a tree at each end of the street. If the distance between every two trees is 10 meters, what is the length of that street?

End-of-Year Test H

Section A

Questions 1 to 15 carry 1 point each. For each question, choose the correct answer and write its letter in the parentheses ( ) provided.

1. $7000 + 100 + 5 = \square$
   a. 7015   b. 7051
   c. 7105   d. 7150   (   )

2. Which is an odd number?
   a. 2390   b. 3475
   c. 4806   d. 7702   (   )

Use the diagram to answer questions 3 and 4.

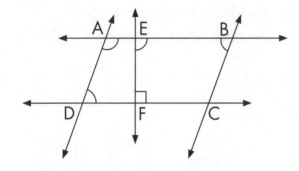

3. Which is a right angle?
   a. ∠BAD   b. ∠ABC
   c. ∠CDA   d. ∠BEF   (   )

4. Which line is perpendicular to $\overleftrightarrow{DC}$?
   a. $\overleftrightarrow{AB}$ b. $\overleftrightarrow{AD}$
   c. $\overleftrightarrow{BC}$ d. $\overleftrightarrow{EF}$ (   )

The bar graph shows the number of books sold by the Peter Pan Book Shop each week. Use the graph to answer questions 5 and 6.

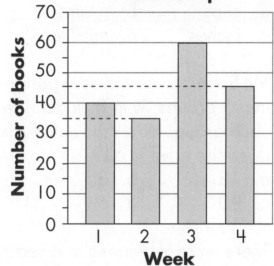

Books sold by Peter Pan Book Shop

5. How many books were sold in Week 2?
   a. 30   b. 35
   c. 40   d. 45   (   )

6. How many more books were sold in Week 3 than in Week 4?
   a. 5   b. 10
   c. 15   d. 20   (   )

7. The table shows the number of people who entered Gym Fitness Center to exercise on three days.

Day	Number of people
Friday	1355
Saturday	2126
Sunday	2220

How many people in all went to the gym over the three days?
a. 5601 b. 5691
c. 5701 d. 5791 ( )

8. Which unit should be used to measure the mass of a box of cereals?
a. cups b. grams
c. inches d. milliliters ( )

9. Ms Sophia's class was separated into 5 groups, with 8 students in each group. How many students does she have in all?
a. 13 b. 35
c. 40 d. 64 ( )

10. There were 9 aviaries in a section at a bird park. There were 130 birds in each aviary. After a few months, 57 birds were removed from the aviaries. How many birds were left?
a. 196 b. 1113
c. 1170 d. 1227 ( )

11. Which figure has more than two angles that are greater than a right angle?

a.   b.

c.   d.

( )

12. Which object has a mass of about 1 kilogram?

a.  b.

c.   d. ◠ ( )

13. The figure is made up of 2-centimeter squares.

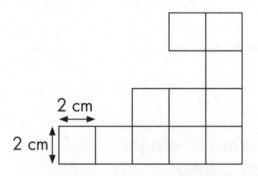

What is the area of the figure?
a. 36 cm² b. 40 cm²
c. 44 cm² d. 48 cm² ( )

14. Lynn started playing basketball at 4.30 p.m. She played for 40 minutes. At what time did she stop playing?
    a. 5.00 p.m.
    b. 5.10 p.m.
    c. 5.20 p.m.
    d. 5.40 p.m.   (   )

15. The clock shows 1 p.m. When it is 4 p.m., what is the angle that the hour hand of the clock has turned?

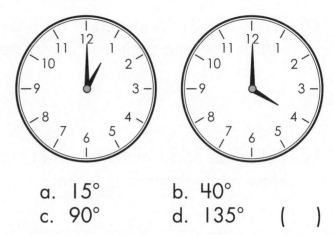

    a. 15°   b. 40°
    c. 90°   d. 135°   (   )

Section B

For questions 16 to 33, each answer carries 1 point.
Write your answer in the answer blank provided.

16. There are 3275 insects in a garden.
    What does the digit 5 in 3275 stand for?

    Ans: _____

17. Bella has 8551 matchboxes in her collection.
    How many thousands is that?

    Ans: _____ thousands

18. $27 \times 7 = \boxed{}$

    Ans: _____

19. What are the missing numbers?

    $$\frac{2}{5} = \frac{4}{\boxed{}} = \frac{8}{\boxed{}} = \frac{\boxed{}}{15}$$

    Ans: _____, _____, _____

20. What is the area of the rectangle?

    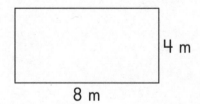

    4 m

    8 m

    Ans: _____ m²

102

Use the figure ABCD to answer questions 21 and 22.

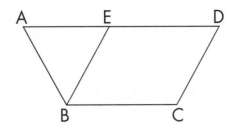

21. How many angles are there within the figure?

Ans: _____

22. Which line segment is parallel to line segment CD?

Ans: _____

23. Which figure is $\frac{3}{8}$ shaded?

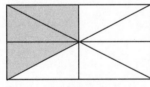

Figure P

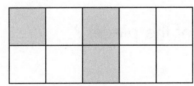

Figure Q

Ans: Figure _____

24. What fraction of the figure is shaded?

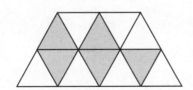

Ans: _____

103

Use the figures M, N, and L to answer questions 25 and 26.

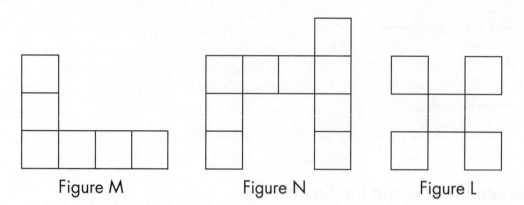

Figure M   Figure N   Figure L

25. Which figure has the smallest area?

Ans: Figure _____

26. Which figure has the smallest perimeter?

Ans: Figure _____

27. A carpet measuring 8 meters by 5 meters is cut
into 4 equal pieces.
What is the total area of 3 of the pieces?

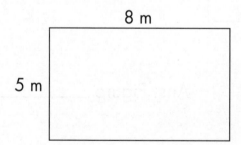

Ans: _____ m^2

28. Mr Kelly put $8\frac{1}{2}$ liters of gasoline in his car.

How many milliliters is that?

Ans: _____ mL

29. A farm has 10 horses and the same number of goats.
There are 4 times as many sheep as horses, and
3 times as many cows as goats.
How many animals are there on the farm?

Ans: _____ animals

30. Mrs Gopal had a box of biscuits.
When she shared them equally among 8 students,
each student received 9 biscuits. If each student
received 8 biscuits instead, how many biscuits
would be left over?

Ans: _____ biscuits

31. The table shows how much maple syrup Chad made
on four days last week.

Day	Maple syrup (liters)
Sunday	$\frac{1}{2}$
Tuesday	$\frac{3}{4}$
Thursday	$\frac{5}{8}$
Saturday	$\frac{1}{3}$

On which day did Chad make the most syrup?

Ans: _____

32. What is the value of Q?

$$\frac{2}{6} = \frac{5}{Q}$$

Ans: _____

33. Arrange the fractions in order. Begin with the greatest.

$$\frac{7}{8}, \frac{5}{6}, \frac{8}{8}, \frac{4}{9}$$

Ans: _____, _____, _____, _____

Section C

For questions 34 to 41, each answer carries 1 point.
Write your answer in the space provided.
Show your work.

34. Jamie used $\frac{3}{4}$ kilogram of brownie mix together with

    $\frac{1}{8}$ kilogram of sugar.

    a. What was the mass of the mixture?
    b. How much more brownie mix than sugar did
       she use?

35. An apartment block has 25 floors with 4 apartments
    on each floor.

    a. How many apartments are there in one block?
    b. How many apartments are there in an estate
       of 45 such blocks?

36. Each box of Builder Blocks contained 36 blocks.
Jim bought 4 boxes of Builder Blocks.

    a. How many Builder Blocks did Jim have?

    b. If Jim separates the blocks equally into 6 piles,
       how many blocks will he have in each pile?

37. Jasper bought 7 cylinders of breadsticks, with
each cylinder containing 250 breadsticks. He then
sold them in packs of 10.
How many packs of breadsticks did Jasper sell?

38. The bar graph shows the brands of cars that were sent to a workshop in a month. Use the graph to answer the questions.

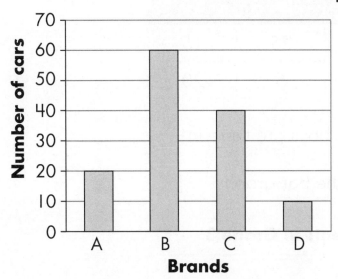

Brands of cars sent to a workshop

a. Which brand were most of the cars?
b. What was the total number cars sent to the workshop?
c. Mr Lim wanted to buy a new car. Based on the graph, which brand would you recommend to him and why?

39. In Progress School, the clerk wanted to know how many boys and girls there were in each Grade 3 class. She placed the information in a table.

Class	3A	3B	3C	3D
Girls	10	15	25	15
Boys	20	15	5	20

a. How many more girls than boys are there in Grade 3?

b. Use the table to complete the bar graph.

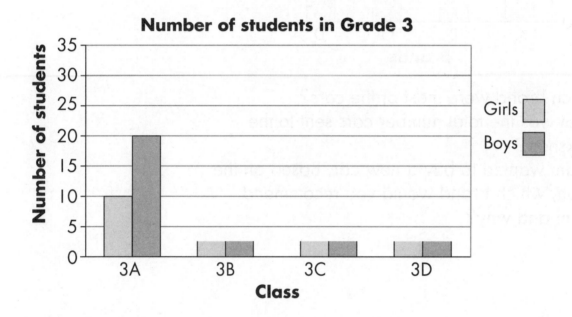

40. On Monday, Joseph attended a talk for $1\frac{1}{2}$ hours.

Then, he spent 25 minutes on a Science worksheet,
15 minutes on English grammar, and 1 hour 30 minutes
on a Mathematics project.
How many more minutes did Joseph spend on
homework than at the talk?

41. Mary wants to decorate her classroom notice board
by attaching a ribbon border around it.
The notice board is made up of two identical squares
and a rectangle.

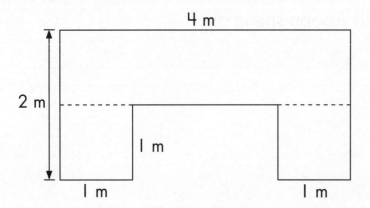

a. What is the length of the ribbon she needs?
b. What is the area of the notice board?

Skills and Strategies Index

Mid-Year Test A

Skills		Knowledge	Comprehension	Application
WHOLE NUMBERS				
1	Number notation and place value	Q1, Q2, Q5, Q16, Q17, Q19	Q20, Q21, Q26, Q27	
2	Addition and subtraction	Q3, Q35(b)	Q13	Q28
3	Multiplication and division by a 1-digit number	Q6, Q7, Q8	Q9, Q10, Q29, Q30	Q33, Q34
4	Odd and even numbers	Q4, Q18	Q31, Q32, Q35(a)	
5	Word problems		Q11, Q12, Q14, Q15, Q22, Q23, Q24, Q25, Q36, Q37, Q38, Q39	Q40, Q41, Q42
Strategies		**Knowledge**	**Comprehension**	**Application**
1	Draw a model		Q36, Q39	Q40, Q41
2	Simplify the problem			Q41, Q42

Mid-Year Test B

Skills		Knowledge	Comprehension	Application
WHOLE NUMBERS				
1	Number notation and place value	Q1, Q2, Q5, Q16, Q17	Q24, Q25, Q28, Q29, Q32, Q33	
2	Addition and subtraction	Q10	Q26, Q27	Q40
3	Multiplication and division by a 1-digit number	Q6, Q8, Q9	Q7, Q19, Q20	Q43
4	Odd and even numbers	Q3, Q4	Q13, Q18, Q30, Q31	
5	Word problems		Q11, Q12, Q14, Q15, Q21, Q22, Q23, Q34, Q36, Q37, Q38, Q39	Q35, Q41, Q42, Q44
Strategies		**Knowledge**	**Comprehension**	**Application**
1	Simplify the problem			Q40
2	Make a systematic list			Q43

Mid-Year Test C

	Skills	Knowledge	Comprehension	Application
WHOLE NUMBERS				
1	Number notation and place value	Q1, Q2, Q4, Q9, Q16, Q18	Q10, Q19, Q22, Q38	Q32, Q33
2	Addition and subtraction	Q5	Q12, Q23	
3	Multiplication and division by a 1-digit number	Q6, Q7, Q8	Q20, Q21, Q26	
4	Odd and even numbers	Q3	Q11, Q17, Q24, Q25, Q38(a)	
5	Word problems		Q13, Q14, Q15, Q27, Q28, Q29, Q30, Q31, Q34, Q35, Q36, Q37	Q39, Q40, Q41
	Strategies	**Knowledge**	**Comprehension**	**Application**
1	Draw a model		Q34	Q39(b), Q40
2	Simplify the problem			Q40

Mid-Year Test D

	Skills	Knowledge	Comprehension	Application
WHOLE NUMBERS				
1	Number notation and place value	Q1, Q2, Q4, Q16, Q17	Q26, Q27, Q28, Q33	
2	Addition and subtraction	Q9, Q19, Q20	Q29, Q30	Q14, Q35
3	Multiplication and division by a 1-digit number	Q5, Q6, Q7, Q8, Q25	Q24	Q34
4	Odd and even numbers	Q3, Q18	Q10, Q21, Q22, Q23	
5	Word problems		Q11, Q12, Q13, Q15, Q31, Q32, Q36, Q37, Q38, Q39	Q40, Q41, Q42, Q43
	Strategies	**Knowledge**	**Comprehension**	**Application**
1	Draw a model		Q38	
2	Simplify the problem			Q41
3	Make a systematic list			Q42
4	Guess and check			Q43

End of-Year Test E

Skills		Knowledge	Comprehension	Application
WHOLE NUMBERS				
1	Number notation and place value	Q2, Q16	Q5, Q17	
2	Addition and subtraction			
3	Multiplication and division by a 1-digit number	Q3, Q4, Q18	Q32	
4	Odd and even numbers	Q1		
5	Word problems		Q12, Q13, Q14, Q20, Q36	Q43
MONEY AND MEASURES				
6	Units of measure			
7	Area and perimeter	Q6, Q25, Q30, Q31		
8	Word problems		Q15, Q37, Q40, Q41, Q42	
STATISTICS				
9	Bar graphs	Q7, Q8, Q28	Q29	
FRACTIONS				
10	Equivalent fractions	Q19, Q26, Q27	Q33	
11	Comparing and ordering		Q34, Q35	
12	Addition and subtraction			
13	Word problems		Q38, Q39	
GEOMETRY				
14	Angles	Q11, Q23		
15	Perpendicular and parallel lines	Q9, Q10, Q21, Q22, Q24		
	Strategy	Knowledge	Comprehension	Application
1	Simplify the problem		Q42	

End of-Year Test F

Skills		Knowledge	Comprehension	Application
WHOLE NUMBERS				
1	Number notation and place value	Q1, Q16, Q17		
2	Addition and subtraction			
3	Multiplication and division by a 1-digit number	Q18		
4	Odd and even numbers	Q2		
5	Word problems		Q8, Q9, Q10, Q32, Q33, Q35, Q37	Q41, Q42
MONEY AND MEASURES				
6	Units of measure	Q25	Q12	
7	Area and perimeter	Q3, Q4, Q26, Q27		
8	Word problems		Q13, Q14, Q15, Q37, Q38, Q40	
STATISTICS				
9	Bar graphs	Q7, Q28	Q29	
FRACTIONS				
10	Equivalent fractions	Q19, Q23, Q24	Q30	
11	Comparing and ordering		Q11, Q31	
12	Addition and subtraction			
13	Word problems		Q34, Q36, Q39	
GEOMETRY				
14	Angles	Q6, Q21, Q22		
15	Perpendicular and parallel lines	Q5, Q20		
Strategy		**Knowledge**	**Comprehension**	**Application**
1	Guess and check			Q42

End of-Year Test G

Skills		Knowledge	Comprehension	Application
WHOLE NUMBERS				
1	Number notation and place value	Q1, Q16, Q17	Q7	
2	Addition and subtraction	Q8		
3	Multiplication and division by a 1-digit number	Q18, Q19	Q30	
4	Odd and even numbers	Q2		
5	Word problems		Q9, Q20, Q34, Q35	
MONEY AND MEASURES				
6	Units of measure	Q12	Q13	
7	Area and perimeter	Q28	Q11, Q26, Q27, Q29	Q33
8	Word problems		Q10, Q14, Q15, Q39	Q40, Q41
STATISTICS				
9	Bar graphs	Q5, Q6	Q25, Q37	
FRACTIONS				
10	Equivalent fractions	Q21, Q23, Q24	Q31	
11	Comparing and ordering		Q32	
12	Addition and subtraction			
13	Word problems		Q36, Q38	
GEOMETRY				
14	Angles	Q4, Q22		
15	Perpendicular and parallel lines	Q3		
Strategies		Knowledge	Comprehension	Application
1	Simplify the problem		Q39	
2	Look for patterns			Q40
3	Make a systematic list			Q40
4	Draw a diagram			Q41

End of-Year Test H

Skills		Knowledge	Comprehension	Application
WHOLE NUMBERS				
1	Number notation and place value	Q1, Q16, Q17		
2	Addition and subtraction	Q7		
3	Multiplication and division by a 1-digit number	Q18		
4	Odd and even numbers	Q2		
5	Word problems		Q9, Q10, Q29, Q30, Q35, Q36, Q37	
MONEY AND MEASURES				
6	Units of measure	Q8	Q12	
7	Area and perimeter	Q20	Q13, Q25, Q26, Q41	
8	Word problems		Q14, Q27, Q28	
STATISTICS				
9	Bar graphs	Q5	Q6, Q38, Q39	
FRACTIONS				
10	Equivalent fractions	Q19, Q23, Q24	Q31, Q32	
11	Comparing and ordering		Q33	
12	Addition and subtraction			
13	Word problems		Q34, Q40	
GEOMETRY				
14	Angles	Q3, Q21	Q11	Q15
15	Perpendicular and parallel lines	Q4, Q22		
Strategy		**Knowledge**	**Comprehension**	**Application**
1	Simplify the problem		Q41	

Answer Key

Mid-Year Test A

Section A

1. c	2. c	3. d	4. b
5. d	6. a	7. d	8. d
9. b	10. c	11. c	12. d
13. b	14. c	15. a	

Section B

16. Eight thousand and ninety-eight

17. 200	18. 1987
19. 8011	20. 28, 37
21. 6000 + 800 + 9	22. 50
23. 48	24. 74
25. 39	26. 700
27. 850	28. 7
29. 12	30. 2
31. 1574	32. 7541
33. 5	34. 40

Section C

35. a. odd number + even number = odd number
    odd number + odd number = even number
    even number + even number = even number
    The two numbers are **778** and **532**.

    b. 147 + 778 + 532 = 1457
    The sum of all three numbers is **1457**.

36. Strategy: Draw a model

    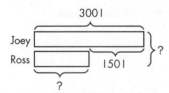

    a. 3001 – 1501 = 1500
    Ross has **1500 stamps**.

    b. 3001 + 1500 = 4501
    They have **4501 stamps** altogether.

37. a. 9871 – 9178 = 693
    The difference in the number of contestants is **693**.

    b. 9871 + 128 = 9999
    The total number of contestants now in the singing competition is **9999**.

38. a. 4560 – 2053 = 2507
    There were 2507 boys in the race.
    2507 – 2053 = 454
    There were **454 more boys** than girls in the race.

    b. 4560 – 3471 = 1089
    1089 students dropped out of the race.

39. Strategy: Draw a model

    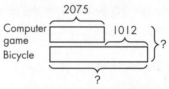

    a. 2075 + 1012 = 3087
    Justin needs **3087 points** to redeem the bicycle.

    b. 2075 + 3087 = 5162
    He needs **5162 points** to redeem both the computer game and the bicycle.

40. a. Strategy: Draw a model

    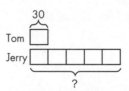

    30 × 5 = 150
    Jerry has **150 stickers**.

b.

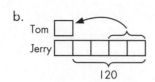

$150 - 30 = 120$
4 units ⟶ 120
1 unit ⟶ $120 \div 4 = 30$
2 units ⟶ $30 \times 2 = 60$
Jerry must give Tom **60 stickers**.

41. a. Strategy: Draw a model / Simplify the problem

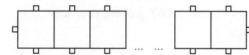

1 mango ⟶ 6 units
3 mangoes ⟶ 18 units
12 pears ⟶ 12 units
3 mangoes and 12 pears ⟶ $18 + 12 = 30$ units
30 units ÷ 6 units = 5
I could have bought **5 mangoes** with the same amount of money.

b. 30 units ÷ 1 unit = 30
I could have bought **30 pears** with the same amount of money.

42. Strategy: Simplify the problem
1 table can seat 4 people.

A corner table can seat 3 people.
2 corner tables can seat $2 \times 3 = 6$ people
$30 - 6 = 24$ people
$24 \div 2 = 12$ tables
$12 + 1 + 1 = 14$ tables
14 tables are needed for 30 people.

Mid-Year Test B

Section A
1. c   2. b   3. a   4. d
5. b   6. d   7. a   8. c
9. d   10. c   11. c   12. c
13. b   14. d   15. d

Section B
16. 6230   17. 70
18. 39, 41, 43   19. 129
20. 10 000   21. 90
22. 540   23. 8
24. 9401   25. 792
26. 800   27. 338
28. 550   29. 4
30. 1265   31. 6512
32. 5265   33. 24
34. 80   35. 25

Section C
36. Total number of people at the rally ⟶ 8925
$8925 - 5928 = 2997$
2997 people arrived at the rally an hour later.

37. a. $2387 + 2207 = 4594$
They picked **4594 apples** altogether.

b. $2387 - 2207 = 180$
Adam picked **180 more apples** than June.

38. a. $3500 - 1109 = 2391$
There were **2391 women** seated at the concert.

b. $3500 + 1340 = 4840$
The total number of people at the concert is 4840.

39. a. $200 + 300 = 500$
$500 \div 5 = 100$
She will have **100 packets** of hair clips.

b. $500 + 130 = 630$
$630 \div 8 = 78 \text{ R}6$
6 hair clips will be left unpacked.

40. Strategy: Simplify the problem
$21 + 39 = 60$
$22 + 38 = 60$
$23 + 37 = 60$
$60 \times 3 = 180$
The sum is **180**.

41. a. $32 \times 9 = 288$
The shop prepared **288 bagels**.

b. $288 - 146 = 142$
$142 \div 7 = 20 \text{ R}2$
2 bagels were not packed into boxes.

42. a. Vicky's age 6 years ago → $14 - 6 = 8$
    $50 - 8 = 42$
    $42 + 6 = 48$
    Vicky's father is **48 years old** now.

    b. $48 + 14 = 62$
    Their total age now is **62 years**.

43. Strategy: Make a systematic list
    Numbers greater than 13 and less than 26:
    14, 15, 16, 17, 18, 19, 20, 21, 22, 23, 24, 25
    Numbers that can be divided by 4: 16, 20, 24
    Numbers that can be divided by 5: 15, 20, 25
    I am the number **20**.

44. a. 7 boxes of cereal → 3 muesli bars free
    ? → 9 muesli bars free
    $9 \div 3 = 3$
    $7 \times 3 = 21$
    She must buy **21 boxes** of cereal.

    b. $42 \div 7 = 6$
    $6 \times 3 = 18$
    She will get **18 muesli bars**.

Mid-Year Test C

Section A
1. d	2. d	3. d	4. d
5. d	6. a	7. d	8. c
9. c	10. a	11. c	12. c
13. d	14. d	15. a	

Section B
16. 300
17. 48, 50, 52, 54
18. 6041
19. $8000 + 70 + 1$
20. 101
21. 41
22. 6098
23. 7158
24. 6619 and 1223
25. 3136 and 1223
26. 15
27. 50
28. 24
29. 9
30. 140
31. 1389
32. 660, 664, or 668
33. 81

Section C
34. Strategy: Draw a model

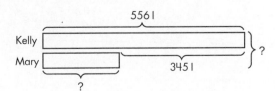

a. $5561 - 3451 = 2110$
   Mary scored **2110 points**.

b. $5561 + 2110 = 7671$
   They scored **7671 points** in total.

35. a. $3459 + 4229 = 7688$
    There are **7688 eggs** in total.

    b. $4229 - 3459 = 770$
    There are **770 more white eggs** than brown eggs.

36. a. $410 \div 8 = 51$ R2
    $$\begin{array}{r} 51 \\ 8 \overline{)410} \\ \underline{40} \\ 10 \\ \underline{8} \\ 2 \end{array}$$
    There were **51 balls** in each basket.

    b. **2 balls** were left behind.

37. a. $6127 - 2167 = 3960$
    The difference in the number of people is **3960**.

    b. $6127 + 873 = 7000$
    There are **7000 people** on board now.

38. a. The greatest 4-digit even number is **6510**.

    b. Greatest 4-digit number: 6510
    Smallest 4-digit number: 1056
    $6510 - 1056 = 5454$
    The difference between the greatest and smallest numbers is **5454**.

39. a. $22 \times 4 = 88$
    Jill has 88 beans.

    b. Strategy: Draw a model

    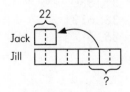

    1 unit → $22 \div 2 = 11$
    2 units → 22
    3 units → $3 \times 11 = 33$
    Jill must give Jack **33 beans**.

40. a. Strategy: Draw a model / Simplify the problem

Book ▢▢▢▢▢
Magazine ▢

I book ⟶ 5 units
5 books ⟶ 5 × 5 = 25 units
I magazine ⟶ I unit
6 magazines ⟶ 6 units
5 books and 6 magazines ⟶ 25 + 6 = 31 units
31 ÷ 5 = 6 R I
I could have bought **6 books** with the same amount of money.

b. 31 ÷ 1 = 31
I could have bought **31 magazines** with the same amount of money.

41. A table can seat 6 people.
A corner table can seat 6 – 1 = 5 people
2 corner tables can seat 5 × 2 = 10 people
26 – 10 = 16 people
16 ÷ 4 = 4 tables in between
4 + 2 = 6 tables
6 tables are needed for 26 people.

Mid-Year Test D

Section A

1. c 2. b 3. c 4. b
5. b 6. c 7. d 8. c
9. d 10. b 11. c 12. a
13. c 14. b 15. d

Section B

16. Five thousand and eleven
17. 7000 18. 102
19. 138 20. 91
21. 4301 22. 2078
23. 76, 78, 80, 82, 84, 86, 88
24. 112 25. 500
26. 7271 27. 450
28. 1000 + 160 + 25 29. 9308
30. 707 31. 380
32. 15 33. 6731
34. 20 35. 6

Section C

36. a. 600 – 235 = 365
365 computers were not destroyed.

b. 365 ÷ 5 = 73
There were **73 crates**.

37. a. I pack of cards ⟶ 2 free stickers
? ⟶ 48 free stickers
48 ÷ 2 = 24
Sophie needs to buy **24 packs** of cards.

b. 24 – 16 = 8
She needs to buy **8 more packs** of cards.

38. Strategy: Draw a model

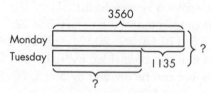

a. 3560 – 1135 = 2425
2425 tarts were baked on Tuesday.

b. 3560 + 2425 = 5985
5985 tarts were baked on both days.

39. I crate ⟶ 40 × 4 = 160 pineapples
7 crates ⟶ 160 × 7 = 1120 pineapples
He packs **1120 pineapples**.

40. a. Minah's age today ⟶ 10 + 8 = 18
60 – 18 = 42
Minah's mother is **42 years** old today.

b. 42 – 8 = 34
34 + 10 = 44
Their total age 8 years ago was **44 years**.

41. a. Strategy: Simplify the problem
6 bars of soap bought ⟶ 2 bars free
36 bars of soap bought ⟶ ? free
36 ÷ 6 = 6
2 × 6 = 12
The customer gets **12 bars** of soap for free.

b. 6 bars of soap + 2 bars of soap
= 8 bars of soap
32 ÷ 8 = 4
6 × 4 = 24
He must buy **24 bars** of soap.

42. a. Strategy: Make a systematic list

| 3 | 6 | 2 | 8 |

3628	3682	3268	3286
3826	3862	6328	6382
6238	6283	6823	6832
2368	2386	2836	2863
2638	2683	8362	8326
8623	8632	8236	8263

She can form **24 different 4-digit numbers**.

b. Greatest 4-digit number: 8632
Smallest 4-digit number: 2368
8632 − 2368 = 6264
The difference between the greatest and smallest
4-digit numbers is **6264**.

43. a. Strategy: Guess and check
Total number of vehicles ⟶ 66
Total number of wheels ⟶ 204
1 car ⟶ 4 wheels
1 motorcycle ⟶ 2 wheels

Total number of vehicles	Number of cars	Number of wheels on cars	Number of motorcycles	Number of wheels on motorcycles	Total number of wheels
66	33	33 × 4 = 132	33	33 × 2 = 66	132 + 66 = 198
66	35	35 × 4 = 140	31	31 × 2 = 62	140 + 62 = 202
66	36	36 × 4 = 144	30	30 × 2 = 60	144 + 60 = 204

There are **30 motorcycles**.

b. 204 − 112 = 92
92 wheels were removed.
Half the cars ⟶ 36 ÷ 2 = 18 cars
18 × 4 = 72 wheels removed
92 − 72 = 20 motorcycle wheels
20 ÷ 2 = 10
There were **10 motorcycles** removed.

End-of-Year Test E

Section A

1. d   2. c   3. b   4. c
5. d   6. b   7. d   8. c
9. d   10. c   11. b   12. b
13. c   14. c   15. c

Section B

16. 300   17. 78
18. 516   19. 8, 15, and 16
20. 442   21. Park Street
22. Gray Road   23. 6
24. 3   25. 4
26. B   27. $\frac{1}{2}$
28. D   29. 3000
30. A, C   31. B, D
32. 6   33. 4
34. 1, $\frac{3}{5}$, $\frac{2}{4}$, $\frac{2}{7}$ 35. $\frac{6}{9}$, $\frac{6}{8}$, $\frac{4}{5}$, $\frac{9}{10}$

Section C

36. a. $736 \times 6 = 4416$
There are **4416 pears** in 6 boxes.

b. $4416 \div 5 = 883 \, R1$
1 pear is left.

37. a. $750 − 260 = 490$
490 grams of flour are left.

b. $490 \div 2 = 245$
The mass of flour in each bag is **245 grams**.

38. a. $\frac{3}{5} + \frac{1}{10} = \frac{6}{10} + \frac{1}{10}$
$= \frac{7}{10}$
They have $\frac{7}{10}$ **liter** of fruit juice altogether.

b. $\frac{7}{10} + \frac{3}{10} = \frac{10}{10}$
$= 1$
They have **1 liter** of fruit juice now.

39. a. $\frac{2}{3} − \frac{1}{6} = \frac{4}{6} − \frac{1}{6}$
$= \frac{3}{6}$
$= \frac{1}{2}$
$\frac{1}{2}$ **liter** of milk was left.

b. $\frac{1}{2} − \frac{1}{12} = \frac{6}{12} − \frac{1}{12}$
$= \frac{5}{12}$
He had $\frac{5}{12}$ **liter** of milk.

40. a. Length = 43 + 43 + 28 + 28
    = 142
    The length of the wire fence is **142 meters**.

    b. Area = 43×28
    = 1204
    The area of the garden is
    1204 square meters.

41. a. 43 min + 1 h 10 min + 24 min + $1\frac{1}{2}$ h
    = 2 h + 43 min + 10 min + 24 min + 30 min
    = 2 h + 107 min
    = 2 h + 1 h + 47 min
    = 3 h 47 min
    She spent **3 hours 47 minutes** on her project altogether.

    b. 1 hour 10 min − 24 min = 70 min − 24 min
    = 46 min
    She spent **46 more minutes** on Tuesday than on Wednesday.

42. Strategy: Simplify the problem
    a. Perimeter = 12 + 8 + 12 + 8
    = 40
    The length of his fence is **40 meters**.

    b. Area of square = 4×4
    = 16 m^2
    Area of rectangle = 12×4
    = 48 m^2
    Area of garden = 16 + 48
    = 64 m^2
    He will need **64 square meters** of carpet grass.

43. $200 \times 4 = 800$
    $800 \div 2 = 400$
    $400 \div 5 = 80$ packs
    $400 \div 8 = 50$ packs
    $80 + 50 = 130$
    He got **130 packs** of keychains.

End-of-Year Test F

Section A
1. b	2. d	3. c	4. c
5. d	6. a	7. c	8. d
9. c	10. c	11. b	12. d
13. d	14. b	15. a	

Section B
16. 70	17. 25
18. 375	19. 16, 6, 20
20. Line DC or $\overleftrightarrow{DC}$	21. 5
22. less than	23. A
24. $\frac{1}{3}$	25. umbrella
26. P, S	27. P, R
28. Red	29. 15
30. 15	31. $\frac{6}{13}, \frac{3}{6}, \frac{3}{4}, \frac{5}{5}$
32. 22	33. 240

Section C
34. a. The highest number of visitors was **4500**.

    b. 4000 − 2000 = 2000
    $2000 \times 2 = 4000$
    The difference is **4000 flowers**.

35. a. 6 boys + 3 girls = 9 students
    $8 \times 9 = 72$
    She gave **72 pencils** to her students in total.

    b. $7 \times 9 = 63$
    72 − 63 = 9
    9 pencils would be left over.

36. a. $\frac{1}{8} + \frac{3}{4} = \frac{1}{8} + \frac{6}{8}$
    $= \frac{7}{8}$
    She made $\frac{7}{8}$ **liter** of fruit punch.

    b. $\frac{3}{4} - \frac{1}{8} = \frac{6}{8} - \frac{1}{8}$
    $= \frac{5}{8}$
    She used $\frac{5}{8}$ **more liter** of water than syrup.

37. $9 \times 7 = 63$
    1 student ⟶ 9 crayons
    9 students ⟶ $9 \times 9 = 81$ crayons
    81 − 63 = 18
    He is short of **18 crayons**.

38. a. Perimeter
    = 5 + 3 + 3 + 3 + 3 + 3 + 5 + 3 + 3 + 3
    = 34 m
    His fence is **34 meters** long.

124

b. Area of one square = 3×3
$\qquad\qquad\qquad = 9 \text{ m}^2$
Area of rectangle = 9×2
$\qquad\qquad\qquad = 18 \text{ m}^2$
Area of playground = $9 + 9 + 18$
$\qquad\qquad\qquad = 36 \text{ m}^2$
He will need **36 square meters** of turf grass.

39. a. $\dfrac{1}{6} - \dfrac{1}{12} = \dfrac{2}{12} - \dfrac{1}{12}$
$\qquad\qquad = \dfrac{1}{12}$

There is $\dfrac{1}{12}$ **kilogram** more sugar than butter.

b. $\dfrac{1}{2} + \dfrac{1}{6} + \dfrac{1}{12} = \dfrac{6}{12} + \dfrac{2}{12} + \dfrac{1}{12}$
$\qquad\qquad\qquad = \dfrac{9}{12}$
$\qquad\qquad\qquad = \dfrac{3}{4}$

The total mass of the mixture is $\dfrac{3}{4}$ **kilogram**.

40. a. Time spent on homework:
$25 \text{ min} + 40 \text{ min} + 1 \text{ h } 30 \text{ min}$
$= 65 \text{ min} + 1 \text{ h } 30 \text{ min}$
$= 1 \text{ h } 5 \text{ min} + 1 \text{ h } 30 \text{ min}$
$= 2 \text{ h } 35 \text{ min}$
Randy spent **2 hours 35 minutes** on all his homework.

b. $2 \text{ h } 35 \text{ min} - 2 \text{ h } 30 \text{ min}$
$= 5 \text{ min}$
Randy spent **5 minutes more** on his homework than on soccer.

41. $4 \times 105 = 420$
$\dfrac{1}{3} \times 420 = 140$
$140 \div 7 = 20 \text{ packs}$
$\dfrac{2}{3} \times 420 = 280$
$280 \div 8 = 35 \text{ packs}$
$20 + 35 = 55$
She had **55 packs**.

42. Strategy: Guess and check
Total number of animals: 20
Total number of legs: 56

Total number of animals	Number of chickens	Number of legs of chickens	Number of sheep	Number of legs of sheep	Total number of legs
20	10	10×2 = 20	10	10×4 = 40	20 + 40 = 60
20	11	11×2 = 22	9	9×4 = 36	22 + 36 = 58
20	12	12×2 = 24	8	8×4 = 32	24 + 32 = 56

There are **12 chickens and 8 sheep**.

End-of-Year Test G

Section A
1. d   2. c   3. b   4. a
5. c   6. c   7. d   8. d
9. c   10. c   11. b   12. c
13. c   14. b   15. d

Section B
16. 1000   17. 176
18. 240   19. 345
20. 70   21. 2, 5, 10
22. 8   23. B
24. $\dfrac{1}{3}$ 25. 480
26. X   27. Z
28. 49   29. 42
30. 12   31. 18
32. $\dfrac{3}{9}, \dfrac{5}{10}, \dfrac{3}{4}, \dfrac{6}{6}$ 33. 138

Section C
34. a. 1 page ⟶ 100 stickers
22 pages ⟶ $100 \times 22 = 2200$ stickers
There are **2200 stickers** in the album.

b. $2200 \div 11 = 200$
He pastes **200 stickers** on each page.

35. a. 1 class ⟶ 38 students
12 classes ⟶ $38 \times 12 = 456$ students
There are **456 students** altogether.

b. 1 class ⟶ 46 students
10 classes ⟶ $46 \times 10 = 460$ students
$460 - 456 = 4$
4 more students need to join the school.

36. a. $\frac{1}{6} + \frac{1}{2} = \frac{1}{6} + \frac{3}{6}$

$= \frac{4}{6}$

$= \frac{2}{3}$

She used $\frac{2}{3}$ **kilogram** of flour in all.

b. $\frac{1}{2} - \frac{1}{6} = \frac{3}{6} - \frac{1}{6}$

$= \frac{2}{6}$

$= \frac{1}{3}$

She used $\frac{1}{3}$ **kilogram** more flour for the pies than the tarts.

37. a. $92 + 36 + 118 + 54 = 300$

300 people from the four towns take the subway altogether.

b.

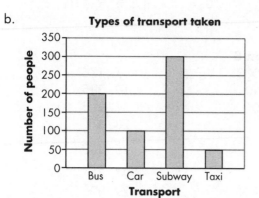

Types of transport taken

38. a. $\frac{1}{4}, \frac{2}{3}, \frac{1}{6}, \frac{3}{4}$

Greatest fraction is $\frac{3}{4}$.

He sold the most lemonade on **Saturday**.

b. $\frac{2}{3} + \frac{1}{6} = \frac{4}{6} + \frac{1}{6}$

$= \frac{5}{6}$

He sold $\frac{5}{6}$ **liter** of lemonade on Thursday and Friday.

39. Strategy: Simplify the problem

a. Perimeter = 25 + 25 + 8 + 8

= 66 cm

She needs **66 centimeters** of ribbon.

b. Area of rectangle = 17×2

= 34 cm²

Area of square = 8×8

= 64 cm²

Area of cardboard = 34 + 64

= 98 cm²

She needs **98 square centimeters** of plastic sheet.

40. a. Strategy: Look for patterns/Make a systematic list

Day	Total length of rope braided	Pattern
1	3 m	
2	5 m	+ 2 m
3	8 m	+ 3 m
4	12 m	+ 4 m
5	17 m	+ 5 m
6	23 m	+ 6 m
7	30 m	+ 7 m
8	38 m	+ 8 m

By the **8th day**, he would have braided 38 meters of the rope.

b.

Day	Total length of rope braided	Pattern
9	47 m	+ 9
10	57 m	+ 10 m
11	68 m	+ 11 m
12	80 m	+ 12 m

The rope was **80 meters** long.

41. Strategy: Draw a diagram

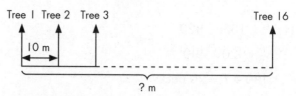

16 − 1 = 15 spaces between trees

15 × 10 m = 150 m

The length of that street is **150 meters**.

End-of-Year Test H

Section A

1. c	2. b	3. d	4. d
5. b	6. c	7. c	8. b
9. c	10. b	11. d	12. a
13. c	14. b	15. c	

Section B

16. 5
17. 8
18. 189
19. 10, 20, 6
20. 32
21. 7
22. $\overline{BE}$
23. P
24. $\frac{5}{12}$
25. L
26. M
27. 30
28. 8500
29. 90
30. 8
31. Tuesday
32. 15
33. $\frac{8}{8}, \frac{7}{8}, \frac{5}{6}, \frac{4}{9}$

Section C

34. a. $\frac{3}{4} + \frac{1}{8} = \frac{6}{8} + \frac{1}{8}$

$= \frac{7}{8}$

The mass of the mixture was **$\frac{7}{8}$ kilogram**.

b. $\frac{3}{4} - \frac{1}{8} = \frac{6}{8} - \frac{1}{8}$

$= \frac{5}{8}$

She used **$\frac{5}{8}$ kilogram** more brownie mix than sugar.

35. a. 1 floor ⟶ 4 apartments
25 floors ⟶ $4 \times 25 = 100$ apartments
There are **100 apartments** in one block.

b. 1 block ⟶ 100 apartments
45 blocks ⟶ $100 \times 45 = 4500$ apartments
There are **4500 apartments** in an estate of 45 such blocks.

36. a. $36 \times 4 = 144$
Jim has **144 Builder Blocks**.

b. $144 \div 6 = 24$
He will have **24 blocks** in each pile.

37. $250 \times 7 = 1750$ breadsticks altogether
$1750 \div 10 = 175$
He had **175 packs** of breadsticks.

38. a. Most of the cars were **Brand B**.

b. $20 + 60 + 40 + 10 = 130$
130 cars were sent to the workshop.

c. **Brand D**, because it had the fewest number of cars sent to the workshop for repairs.

39. a. Number of girls in Grade 3:
$10 + 15 + 25 + 15 = 65$
Number of boys in Grade 3:
$20 + 15 + 5 + 20 = 60$
Difference between the number of girls and boys:
$65 - 60 = 5$
There are **5 more girls** than boys in Grade 3.

b.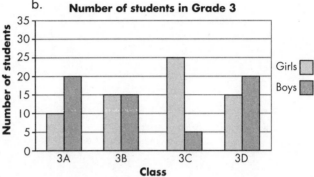

40. Time spent on homework:
25 min $+ 15$ min $+ 1$ h 30 min
$= 40$ min $+ 1$ h 30 min
$= 1$ h 70 min
$= 2$ h 10 min

2 h 10 min $- 1\frac{1}{2}$ h
$= 2$ h 10 min $- 1$ h 30 min
$= 1$ h 70 min $- 1$ h 30 min
$= 40$ min
Joseph spent **40 more minutes** on homework than at the talk.

41. Strategy: Simplify the problem
a. Perimeter $= 4 + 2 + 4 + 2 + 1 + 1$
$= 14$ m
She needs **14 meters** of ribbon.

b. Area of rectangle $= 4 \times 1$
$= 4$ m^2
Area of 1 square $= 1 \times 1$
$= 1$ m^2
Area of cardboard $= 4 + 1 + 1$
$= 6$ m^2
The area of the notice board is **6 square meters**.